THE BEST
LESSON
SERIES:
LITERATURE

15 MASTER
TEACHERS
Share What Works

THE BEST LESSON SERIES: LITERATURE

15 MASTER TEACHERS
Share What Works

Edited by Brian Sztabnik

a Talks with Teachers Publication

Talks with Teachers Media
53 Babylon Drive
Sound Beach, NY 11789

© Copyright 2015 by Brian Sztabnik

ISBN 13 978-0-692-53155-6

Editor: *Brian Sztabnik*
Copy Editor: *Ruth Arseneault*
Cover Design: *Rob Allen*
Contributors: *Ruth Arseneault, Susan Barber, Laura Bradley, Brianna Crowley, Gerard Dawson, Todd Finley, Joy Kirr, Jori Krulder, Shanna Peeples, Amy Rasmussen, Dan Ryder, Josh Stock, Dave Stuart Jr., Brian Sztabnik, Heather Wolpert-Gawron*

For information, contact:

www.talkswithteachers.com

www.bestlessonseries.com

Acknowledgements

"As I teach, I project the condition of my soul onto my students, my subject, and our way of being together."

—Parker J. Palmer
The Courage to Teach: Exploring the Inner Landscape of a Teacher's Life

THIS BOOK IS the result of the creative energy of just a few of the great teachers in the *Talks with Teachers* community. Todd Finley and I first conceived of the idea during a late night phone call. We were brainstorming ways that *Talks with Teachers* could infuse more creativity and joy in classrooms. My wife Jessica, a teacher herself, endured countless questions about format, organization, design, and the Oxford comma. A trusted teacher, Ruth Arseneault, who is the most thoughtful member of the Talks with Teacher Voxer group, edited this book. Special thanks goes to Mark Barnes of *Brilliant or Insane* and Jennifer Gonzalez of *Cult of Pedagogy* for their time, experience, and thoughts throughout the process.

It has been a labor of love, with teachers involved in every step of the way.

In these pages you will find a part of each teacher's soul. It is our way of bringing our love of the classroom, our students, and literature to you.

I remember, though, at one point asking my cooperating teacher, "Is this it? Is this all there is to teaching? What else do you do with a lesson?"

At the moment, I was staring down the next 30 years of my career and had the realization that it might be rinse, wash, repeat, for decades. The thought was dreadful. After all, the structure of school encourages repetition and uniformity — desks in rows, bells ringing on schedule, alphabetical order, single-file lines, and everything else that keeps the ball rolling smoothly.

I yearned for more creative ways to make the text come alive. I wanted more captivating ways to teach literary terms than a textbook glossary. I wanted my classroom to be a magical place of inquiry, discussion, analysis, and development.

Over the next few years I went to work studying creativity, pedagogy, and presentation. I spent time in the classrooms of master teachers and read the biographies of innovators and creatives. I experimented with techniques and approaches, expanding my teacher toolkit and elevating my craft.

Perhaps you have been there too. Perhaps you want something more than scripted lessons and the same-old approach.

Luckily, help is available.

This is a book for teachers who aspire to conquer the repetition. This is a book about what is possible when teachers use creativity to challenge the routine. This is a book that honors great literature by pairing it with activities and learning environments that do justice to the artistry of the works.

As F. Scott Fitzgerald said, "That is part of the beauty of all literature. You discover that your longings are universal longings, that you're not lonely and isolated from anyone. You belong."

Fifteen master teachers have contributed their best literature lesson so that your teaching can have new dimensions, new life. The ideas, approaches, and techniques employed are particular to the works of literature they use, but they are also universal to the principles of good teaching. Many of the lessons are student-centered. Many allow for collaboration so that deeper learning can occur. Many draw on traditional techniques like oral readings, images, and graphic organizers, but do so in novel ways.

It turns out a lesson is quite a nimble thing.

Brian Sztabnik

Editor's Note

THIS BOOK WAS created with students in mind.

It does not follow the typical lesson-plan format. It does not favor educational jargon and buzzwords. It was written with passion and love by 15 master teachers that want to share what has worked so well for them.

Each lessons has been tested in real classrooms with students of all levels and capabilities. They have been honed over the years, resulting in engaged students, intense discussions, critical thinking and outbursts of creativity. They represent the best literature lessons from a select group of master teachers. And now they are yours to make your own.

How the Book is Formatted

In each chapter you will find:

- The story of the lesson's inspiration.

- A backwards-designed lesson plan that emphasizes student learning, not abstract standards.

- Handouts, links, and resources.

- A reflection on what made the lesson memorable.

Go to www.bestlessonseries.com for all handouts and resources.

Table of Contents

Finding Courage to Fly Close to the Sun: Interpreting Icarus

Ruth Arseneault

"I once had a theatre mentor tell me that she saw her job, not as building actors, but as building audiences. That is how I see my English classes. So few of them will go on to become English majors, but by heavens, I want them to continue to experience the joys of deep reading, regardless of what text they encounter. I also want them to have the ability to move through the world experiencing the joys of art and culture, but always with a critical eye."

MY STUDENTS STINK at reading poetry. They avoid it, they rush through it, they make wild conjectures based on... well, sometimes I'm not sure what, frankly. My students are smart cookies. They really are. Its just that many of them come to me with an abhorrence of poetry after having limited experience with it, most of which involves answering teacher-generated questions, labeling literary devices, and feeling frustrated. They rarely have the skills to attack a poem on their own without the help, and often the direct interference, of a teacher. No wonder they don't like it.

I was feeling increasingly guilty about jamming my interpretations down students' gullets like they were *foie gras* geese, and about sending them out into the world without attitudes and skills that I feel are essential to living a good, examined life. I wanted them to like poetry, not just tolerate it. Something had to be done.

The work of Sheridan Blau, Francine Artichuk, and Sarah Brown Wessling helped me find an answer. Blau's seminal book *The Literature Workshop: Teaching Texts and Their Readers* encouraged me to allow the students to take over the work of reading poetry. Instead of having all the fun myself, they should experience the joys of unwrapping a poem's gift of meaning and reaching epiphanies. His work also inspired me to use the Icarus texts as the basis for this learning plan.

Artichuk was a beloved English guru in our district and my mentor when I began teaching. She was teaching lessons twenty years ago based on ideas and methods that some people are only now beginning to adopt. Her joy for teaching at the end of her career surpassed that of most idealistic beginning teachers. Art was often a central feature in her lessons, appealing to the visual learners and artists and historians among her students. She reinforced my love of art and ekphrastic poetry, but more than this, she encouraged me to think like the students do.

As with many teachers, my best ideas are "stolen" from someone else. There are few teachers who inspire this reverent thievery like Sarah Brown Wessling. If you are not familiar with her work, go directly to www.theteachingchannel.org and watch her teach. Do not pass "Go," do not collect $200. What a teacher! Her lesson on basic analysis forms the crux of my lesson. Watch her do it first, and better, here: https://www.teachingchannel.org/videos/teach-students-to-think. I've used a painting instead of an advertisement, and I've jiggled with parts, but this is really her process.

I'm not crazy enough to suggest that this series of lessons will turn a poetry-despiser into a poetry enthusiast, but it does give students the basic skills they need to begin to unpack a poem on their own. One of the unit's strengths is the amount of support students get as they move through the process: from the teacher, from their peers, from the visual component, from the system itself. I have scaffolded this series of lessons so that they get increasingly challenging, but students should always be inside the zone of proximal development. We begin with teacher-led group analysis of a visual to model the three-stage process. The next lesson moves on to individual work. It is with the less rigorous aspects of analyzing a simple poem mixed with peer work on the more cognitively challenging aspects of it. Don't worry, there is a class "check in" for accuracy. Finally, the students work with a more complex poem where they do the analysis with peer support and "check in" with the class for accuracy.

LEARNING PLAN
DAY 1

- Ask students "What is a text?" Answers usually point to written texts – words on a page. Explain that a text is anything that can be read and interpreted.

- Ask for examples of their favorite movies and help them see that an audience "reads" a film or television show. (*Star Wars*, for example, is a stellar example of a heroic journey; "The Walking Dead" can be seen as a commentary on modern fears about social alienation; films have plots, characters, symbols, just as stories do.)

- Move on from here to consider other texts that are less obvious. I have students read and interpret my classroom, my clothing, our cafeteria and its clusters of cliques. I insist that students verbally list what is observable before they try to interpret (the reason for this will become evident later).

- Write three categories on the board: **(1) Observe (2) Find Patterns (3) Draw Conclusions**. Explain that we are going to be reading a visual text and that the process for making thoughtful and thorough readings involves these three steps. As we observe the text, students will first simply look at it and notice what is there.

- Project Pieter Bruegel the Elder's *Landscape With the Fall of Icarus* on the screen. Tell students the painting's title and ask them to divide the image into imaginary quadrants and to look closely at what is in each quadrant. Give them a few seconds to consider the painting and then ask them to say – very objectively – what they observe in the top left quadrant. Ensure that students give literal answers, insisting that they hold off on inferring about its content until later. Students will mention a blue sky, cliffs or mountains, water, and so on. Go on to the top right quadrant, bottom left quadrant, and finish with the bottom right quadrant. It's important to finish with the bottom right, as this is where Icarus is just visible, his feet flailing at the water, and students often miss this tiny detail if they have not been encouraged to examine the rest of the painting's details minutely.

- Sometimes students will have questions about what they see. For example, they may not be familiar with the peasant's dress or what he is doing. Answer these questions, explaining that, like a written text, it is sometimes necessary to fill in background knowledge to help comprehension; it's also important to be familiar with the visual "vocabulary" of a text.

- Once students have exhausted the literal details of the painting, ask them if they can find some patterns in the list they've created. Help students to see that grouping details together will allow them to consider aspects of the painting that a literal list does not. For example, there are will be a great number of words concerning the geographical features of the image, Icarus and the peasant are the only human figures, the plough and ship are man-made objects. As students find patterns, circle the terms that belong to each one and write down the pattern's label.

- Tell students that once they've begun to notice connections and interactions between parts of the text, they're ready to begin considering what these dynamics mean. This is where a reader begins to interpret the text, drawing conclusions about its message. Ask them if they know the story of Icarus, who defied his father, the creator Daedalus, by flying too close to the sun and falling to his death in the sea. Point out that the painting has a plot – there is a story being told in the details.

- Students sometimes have a difficult time moving into interpretation, and they will need support and modeling at this point. Have them take five minutes to free-write about the painting, addressing any aspect of its details or patterns that they find interesting or confusing.

- After five minutes, have students pair/share any interesting idea that came up in their free-writing and then offer one idea up for whole class consideration, or, if students are relatively comfortable in discussions already, they can skip the pair/share and go directly to the whole class discussion.

- As a way of extending their thinking, if these ideas have not been broached already, ask them why the painter would include so many geographical details? What country is represented? What is the significance of the bright, beautiful weather? These details are all important to the plot, but more than this, they construct setting and mood. Another pattern to recognize is that the only moving things in the painting are the ship, the peasant and his horse, and Icarus. These all represent human endeavors – the ploughing and sailing are everyday life, its work, its mundane ordinariness. Icarus' fall is "outside" this pattern as an unusual occurrence because the story indicates how seldom humans truly look outside the ordinary, and how risky it is to do so. Both the peasant and his horse have their backs to the viewer, the peasant's facelessness indicating his lack of individuality: he could be anyone, caught up in everyday concerns, focused solely on what is directly in front of him.

- At the end of the lesson, show to students that the three categories – make observations, find patterns, draw conclusions – correspond to the way we read. When making observations a reader constructs the *literal* meaning, the *text*; when finding patterns a reader must make *inferences*, putting details together to examine the *context*; when drawing conclusions a reader *interprets* the whole text to determine its *subtext*.

- Finish the class by having students write in their notebooks an answer to the question "What did I learn about reading a text?"

DAY 2

- Have students read their answer from their last day's end-of-class writing as a brief review.

- Write on the board the three categories from the previous day: **Make Observations**, **Find Patterns**, **Draw Conclusions**.

- Tell students that they are going to practice this reading process, this time using a written text instead of a visual text. They will be working in their "home groups" (previously established groups of four students) for part of the work, but first they need to do a bit of thinking as individuals. Hand out copies of William Carlos Williams's "Landscape With the Fall of Icarus," one per student.

- Ask students to read the poem through and notice whatever it is they notice. They need not worry about what it "means" at all.

- Students then will highlight nouns corresponding to objects, people, or places in the poem. Next, circle any words that describe these nouns. Draw a line under any actions that are occurring. Put a star next to anything else that seems like it might be important.

- Give each home group a large sheet of paper. Have them put the word "OBSERVATIONS" at the top of the page. On the top half of the page, students make a list of every literal observation they noted in the poem. Circulate around the room to ensure that groups are on track and that they are not jumping ahead and making inferences. This is very difficult for some students, who are used to leaping into interpretation before they have fully considered the text.

- Have students silently consider their lists, looking for similarities, connections, and differences for a few minutes. Then, groups can begin to circle items on the page that correspond to patterns they have found. They can "keep it simple" at this point if they are having difficulties – circle all the characters, geographical features, objects, and label them.

- Bring students back to a whole-class discussion. Ask each group to name one pattern they found and tell what words are associated with that pattern. List the patterns on the board. As a class, consider what each of these patterns might mean, drawing conclusions about their significance. Some possibilities are: there is a pattern of being insignificant/unnoticed that highlights obliviousness to suffering; words associated with joyful springtime (spring, tingling, pageantry) contrast with the central action of Icarus' fall to show irony; the natural world is personified (the ocean is concerned with itself, the year is awake, tingling), perhaps to highlight the universal indifference characteristic of Bruegel's representation of Icarus' story.

- Ask students if they would be able to understand this poem if they were not familiar with Bruegel's painting. (Some will say yes, some no.) This will show students that sometimes a lack of background knowledge will trip up a reader and limit the ability to make meaning of a text.

- Return to the three steps of the reading process that students have practiced: make observations, find patterns, and draw conclusions. Point out to the students how they competently followed this process to make meaning of this poem, giving specific comments and actions that you observed while the students worked:

- *"Remember when Joe said that there were five separate actions in the poem? He didn't stop to think about what they meant, he was just making observations about the literal content. That's a good strategy, because it prevents you from getting caught up in speculation before you have examined the whole text."*

- *"When you told me that there was 'something funny' about the way the natural world was represented, but you didn't know what it was, you were beginning to define a pattern. It's okay to make an initial comment like that and hold off to label it until you think about it a bit more. Be patient with yourselves as you are learning this process."*

- *"When I pushed you to consider Mary's comment that 'No one and nothing cares about Icarus,' I was trying to help you see that drawing a conclusion sometimes takes a great deal of thinking, that it doesn't always come easily. Again, be patient with yourselves through this process."*

- At the end of the class, have students take a few minutes to free-write about this poem, addressing anything they found of interest, any difficulty or frustration, any questions they still have.

DAY 3

- Remind students of Bruegel's painting of Icarus. Put it up on the screen again so students can have a look at it. Ask them what qualities they notice in the painting that might be an

RUTH ARSENEAULT

indication of the artist's style. List their ideas on the board. It's not important what they say, so long as they are considering the painting. (I help students remember this activity later in the term when they begin to analyze an author's style.) Tell them by the end of the class that they will see some others of Bruegel's paintings so they can see if their ideas were accurate.

- Hand out individual copies of W. H. Auden's "Museé des Beaux Arts." Ask students to consider the title: what does it mean? (Art gallery, or fine arts museum.)

- Have students individually read through the poem and take note of any words or phrases that they do not understand. As a class, discuss the meanings of these vocabulary concerns. "The Old Masters" will probably come up – ensure that students understand about artists who are called "Old Masters" by naming a few of them.

- Follow the reading procedure that they used the previous day: ask students simply to read the poem through and notice whatever it is they notice. They need not worry about what it "means" at all. Students then will highlight nouns corresponding to objects, people, or places they notice in the poem. Next, circle any words that describe these nouns. Draw a line under any actions that are occurring.

- This time, ask them to put a star next to anything that indicates the speaker's opinion or perspective. For example, the first sentence "About suffering they were never wrong, / The Old Masters" clearly shows an opinion about the Old Masters.

- This time, students will find and label patterns individually on their copies of the poem. They need not write a list of all the items they observed (some students may still wish to do so – this is fine), but they do need to list the patterns they found.

- Have students check with their home groups once all are finished listing patterns. On a sheet of paper, students collate all their responses.

- Have groups choose two of these patterns from which to draw conclusions. As students discuss possible conclusions, circulate to offer support, asking questions to prod further thinking and pointing out to students when they are doing good thinking by highlighting what students say:

  - *"Hey, did you hear what you said there? 'This speaker sees suffering in artwork.' You just started drawing an important conclusion about the theme of the poem. Can any of you others add to this idea?"*

  - *"Wow – you're really looking at specific details to find evidence for your ideas."*

- Bring students back to a whole-class format. Ask them if they still have questions about the poem. Answer any questions that seem to be inhibiting literal comprehension.

- Discuss the conclusions that groups have considered, looking at specific details from the poem that support each. Sometimes students will have an "off the wall" conclusion. Gently lead them to try and find evidence that supports it. Point out that sometimes a reader has to do "draft copy" readings, adjusting and revising thinking as they consider more deeply. That is part of the process. They must always remember, though, to consider the text as a whole and whether the conclusion logically follows from the available evidence.

- If no one has mentioned that the speaker describes paintings in this poem, help students to notice this in the way details are grouped into sections (like paintings in a *museé des beaux arts*). Remind them of the importance of background knowledge – being familiar with these paintings will add depth to a reading of the poem. Read the poem aloud (or have a good student reader do so). At the same time, project images of paintings by Bruegel similar to those that Auden describes. Pause after each description so students can examine the image and find the specific details Bruegel mentions.

- Have students take a look at the list of characteristics of Bruegel's artwork that they listed on the board. Each student considers this list, revising it mentally. In their notebooks, students write two to three sentences describing Bruegel's style.

- Finish the class by discussing briefly why Auden chose Bruegel's work to illustrate the poem's theme that suffering is a part of everyday life. (Bruegel is noted for his representation of everyday peasant life, having transposed the characters and settings of Greek myths and Biblical stories into those of his own time. His works are filled to the brim with actions and color, so much so that tiny but important details may go unobserved.)

- Often, in a subsequent lesson I'll go on to pair others of William Carlos Williams's poems with their counterparts in the works of Bruegel. Try using William Carlos Williams's "The Peasant Dance" or "The Dance" with Bruegel's *The Peasant Dance*.

HANDOUTS/RESOURCES

Landscape With the Fall of Icarus by Pieter Bruegel
"Landscape With the Fall of Icarus" by William Carlos Williams
"Museé des Beaux Arts" by W. H. Auden

Other Paintings by Pieter Bruegel:

The Triumph of Death
Death of the Virgin
The Adoration of the Magi in the Snow
The Slaughter of the Innocents
Dulle Griet
The Peasant Dance

Reading a Text

Make observations	Find patterns	Draw conclusions
Text	*Context*	*Subtext*
Determine literal meaning	Make internal text connections	Interpret and analyze
What's "on the page"?	What's similar? Dissimilar? Alone?	What does this mean?

WHAT MADE IT **MEMORABLE**

I love the feeling of a classroom where the students are working intently. Even if they're silent, there is a palpable energy in the room that is never, ever there when I stand at the front of the room. This process inspires that kind of focus.

Students love the story of Icarus, the teenage rebel who defied his father, Daedalus, to fully experience the joy of the moment. He died as a result but achieved renown. They relate to him. Of course they do: witness the spate of "jackassery" inspired by reality television. It's not a stretch for students to imagine Icarus saying, "Hey, here are

RUTH ARSENEAULT

of her life — literature — she soon realized that teaching young adults would become an even greater passion. Having started her teaching career at 35, she is grateful that she still has a loooong way to go until retirement because she knows there is no more challenging or fulfilling endeavor than teaching young people. Even after seventeen years, every new day, every new school year provides an opportunity to improve her teaching practice and relationships with students.

Follow her on Twitter @Drama__chick.

The American Dream

Susan Barber

"I want students to understand the idea of the American Dream and have a sense of how varied the dream is among different people throughout different time periods. Students will also comprehend how the arts, not just literature, reflect current events and be able to identify common themes and ideas reflected in the arts."

THIS PICTURE AND the story behind it changed my life. The boy on the left is my husband's grandfather when he was 15 years old; the boy on the right is his 17-year old brother. This was taken their last night in Germany before they set sail for the United States. Their 19-year old brother had gone ahead to the "Land of Opportunity" a few months before and now the younger siblings were following him. Their mother put them on a ship knowing that the state of Germany offered a grim outlook for young men while America offered hope, possibility, and a future. She gave each a small braided piece of her hair and kissed them goodbye knowing she would never see them again. Why would a mother do this?

The American Dream.

I choose to start my year with an image followed by a story. Stories and images are timeless hooks for any generation, so I turn to these to start most lessons, but especially the first lesson of the year. I love to share this story in particular with students because the main characters are boys my students' age so there's immediate interest and relatability. The lesson quickly moves to music clips and visual art, also great hooks for students. Using the arts almost always proves to be a way to pull students into the lesson; it's almost like a trick.

American literature is my sweet spot. I know it backwards and forwards, and for many years taught it chronologically; however, I realized that I was failing to give my students the big picture because I was so caught up in getting through the content, which I never had time to do anyway. I now choose to introduce American literature with a lesson on the American Dream, a theme which can be traced throughout the course, always using it as an anchor. In addition, this lesson introduces the skills of close reading, creating a digital presentation, and writing, so from the very beginning of the year the class has an academic focus.

My goal is for every lesson to be EPIC (experiential, participatory, image driven, and content rich), and this lesson encompasses each of these. Students experience the American Dream through different arts, participate in family groups to understand and discuss concepts, are immediately captured by an image of boys their age, and are exposed to content rich texts. I love starting all-in and moving forward every day from there.

The American Dream
LEARNING GOALS

SUSAN BARBER

BROAD **IMPLICATIONS**

Students will understand that:

- The American Dream is different for different people and dependent upon historical events.

- Literature is just one aspect of the arts.

- One theme can be central in different texts and across different time periods.

- Close reading is helpful in understanding complex texts and identifying theme.

KNOWLEDGE GAINED

Students will know:

- The origins of the American Dream.

- How and why the American Dream has changed.

- How to identify and use evidence from a text to support an idea.

- How to analyze evidence from a text.

- How to create a multimedia presentation.

SKILLS ACQUIRED

Students will be able to:

- Trace a theme over several different time periods in American history.

- Close read a text for evidence relating to a theme.

- Use different sources to form a definition of the American Dream.

- Identify the American Dream in a song, image, and text.

- Create a visual and oral digital presentation of the American Dream.

EVIDENCE OF LEARNING

- Students will develop a working definition of the American Dream from their sources.

- Students will annotate texts for evidence of the American Dream.

- Students will create a digital presentation of their American Dream featuring music, visual art, literature, and an original piece.

- Students will write reflection pieces that go along with the choices in the multi-media presentation.

- Students will present their presentation to the class (optional).

- Students will write synthesis essays about different aspects of the American Dream based on the assigned texts (optional).

LEARNING PLAN

DAY 1

- Show students an image chosen by the teacher and ask students what they think the picture is about. I use the image mentioned at the beginning. After hearing a few answers, I tell them the story of how my husband's grandfather immigrated to the U.S. Any story or image can be used, but personal stories usually work best.

- Students will write their definition of the American Dream on a sticky note and put it on the board. The teacher will read randomly selected student definitions and discuss them with the class.

- The class will watch 3-4 music videos about the American Dream and discuss how the video reflects the American Dream. Videos used in the past have included:

  - "America the Beautiful" sung by Bon Jovi (https://youtu.be/HqHIuzmFXzU)

  - "Coming to America" by Neil Diamond (https://youtu.be/9ttDUGM-1mU)

  - "Chicken Fried" by the Zac Brown Band (https://youtu.be/e4ujS1er1r0)

  - "No Cats in America" from *An American Tale* (https://youtu.be/1_4kU9cwgXM)

  - "Little Pink Houses" by John Cougar Mellancamp (https://youtu.be/qOfkpu6749w)

  The teacher can choose any videos appropriate for the class.

- The class will then view 3-4 paintings related to the American Dream and discuss them. Paintings used in the past have included *American Gothic* by Grant Wood, *Freedom from Want* by Norman Rockwell, *The Problem We all Live With* by Norman Rockwell, *Indian Scout* by Alfred Jacob Miller, and *9:45 a.m. Stratford, Conn.* by Edward Henry.

- Students will write their own definition of the American Dream, which will be shared with their family groups (typically four students randomly assigned). Students should consider various elements of the American Dream that were discussed in class.

SUSAN BARBER

DAY 2

- Students are given four texts – "I Hear America Singing" by Whitman, "The Gift Outright" by Frost, "Let America Be America Again" by Langston Hughes, and an excerpt from *Letters from an American Farmer* by Crevecoeur; however, any texts reflecting the American Dream may be used.

- The teacher will give time-period context for each of the texts, giving enough information for students to be able to draw conclusion on how it relates to the American Dream. Each text will be read aloud in class, and students will choose two to four (depending on the level of the student or class) to annotate for the remainder of the class period and homework, if necessary.

- Since this lesson is done the first week of school, I review how to annotate by modeling it with one of the texts I typically annotate "The Gift Outright" with students since this is the most difficult of the texts. Students may work with partners in their family groups.

DAY 3

- Students will share observations from the texts, work through any questions in family groups, and discuss guiding questions in their family groups. Questions could include:

    - *"What do the lines 'The land was ours before we were the lands' and 'And forthwith found salvation in surrender' from 'The Gift Outright' mean? Why does Frost use the words 'unstoried, artless, unenhanced,' and do these words describe what the land has become?"*

- *"How is 'I Hear America Singing' reflective of Whitman's time period? How does Whitman's use of free verse enhance the overall theme of the poem?"*

- *"Are the inequalities addressed in 'Let America be America Again' resolved? Why or why not? How does Hughes use parenthesis to enhance the overall theme of the poem?"*

- *"How is love for America today different than the love for America described in 'This is an American,' and how do different American Dreams play a role the different ways Americans love their country?"*

- *"What differences can be noted in the mood of each text? Tone? Support for these? What are some possible reasons for the differences?"*

OPTIONS FOR DAY 3

- The teacher may choose to annotate each text as a class with a document camera, which can be beneficial for lower-level classes who are still learning how to read and analyze texts with regard to theme. Upper level classes may choose to have a class discussion on the American Dream, its portrayal in the arts, and the state of the Dream in today's society.

- Students will create a digital presentation of the American Dream featuring music, visual art, literature, and an original piece. (See **Handout 1**.) This presentation must show thoughtful insight and go further than surface level observations. Presentations will be shared in class at a later date. I sometimes do these all in a day or divide them over a couple of weeks.

- Extension essay for upper level classes or students: Students will write an essay showing how the American Dream is reflected throughout different time periods in American history. The essay must include quotations from the texts as well as analysis of the evidence. This writing will serve as a baseline essay for personal writing portfolios.

HANDOUTS/RESOURCES

"The Gift Outright" by Robert Frost
"I Hear America Singing" by Walt Whitman
"Let America be America Again" by Langston Hughes

Handout 1

The American Dream Digital Presentation
American Dream Definition
In a well-developed paragraph define the American Dream and what the dream means to you.

Music
   Select one song that was read in class and that reflects your definition of the American Dream. The lyrics can either respond positively to the dream or react against the dream. Write one paragraph about the song, connecting the lyrics to some aspect of the American Dream.

Art
   Select an image (painting, photograph, drawing) that reflects an aspect of the American Dream. In a well-developed paragraph, explain the connection between the selected image and the American Dream. Your explanation must be more than surface level observations.

Literature
   Select a piece of literature (poem, essay, short story, or novel) that explores the idea of the American Dream. Write a reflection detailing the evidence in the text and how it supports or reacts against the

American Dream. Your reflection should be a minimum of 500 words and should include quotations from the text.

Create

Create an art form relating to your definition of the American Dream. You may write a song, draw a picture, create a collage, paint a painting, write a poem, or use any other medium you chose. The work should be clearly connected to your definition of the American Dream and should be of a quality that shows time, effort, and thoughtful attention were given in its creation.

Present

Prepare a presentation with a multimedia component to be presented to the class, and which includes a portion of your chosen song, the image, the text with at least one quotation from the text, and the art you created. The created portion may be presented live to the class. Your presentation should include an explanation of why the work was chosen with each element.

Please create your digital presentation using a platform that can be shown in class and accessed by the teacher. In addition, please either turn in a hard copy of written paragraphs or submit them online to me by the due date. As always, give credit where credit is due and cite sources.

WHAT MADE IT **MEMORABLE**

Students tend to love this lesson because its focus is the big picture. I think sometimes teachers are so focused on skill development that we lose sight of the large, overall themes resonating throughout content areas. Students also love the incorporation of the arts and are often pulled into the lesson without even realizing it. The discussion of the songs and visual art gives students a chance to practice finding evidence and analyzing it in regard to a specific theme; this warms them up with the skills they will be using during the close reading of texts. I love that students walk away from this lesson considering the lyrics of songs on the radio or scenes from movies seen over the weekend and wondering what statement their writers are trying to make about current society.

Students also walk away with different understandings of the American Dream. At the beginning of the lesson, many students associate the dream with money and/or fame but grow to realize it is much more than this. I love seeing their minds stretch and develop their own ideas about their dreams and their definitions of success.

I love this as a teacher for several reasons. First, I am able to assess my students' ability to find evidence and analyze evidence, which helps me know where to start with specific instruction in close reading. I am also able to assess writing skills at the very beginning of the year and use this as a base for writing instruction. This lesson establishes an atmosphere of community, encouragement, and support because students share projects orally, forcing them to get in front of the class and get talking early in the year. Barriers are broken down early by having students work in randomly chosen family groups in the first lessons and fears of speaking in class are addressed immediately so we can move forward to cooperative and collaborative learning. The concepts of this lesson are transferrable to any theme or any content area by simply finding music, visual art, and literature to reinforce the concepts needing to be taught.

Most importantly for me, this lesson helps me connect with students because I learn so much about them. I learn what type of music they like, how they are wired creatively, if they are shy or over-the-top, and I get to hear many of their stories — stories of students who have moved here from other countries for a better life, stories of how the American Dream has gone bad for their families and their responses to these circumstances, stories of students who have no idea that others in our country don't have luxuries they do. I hear dreams of being a first-generation college student, a legacy at a prestigious school, or a successful entrepreneur. There are dreams of being a teacher, doctor, engineer, and mom. So, more than the instructional value of this lesson, which I do believe is important, I begin the year forming a relationship with my students and gaining insight into their lives, which helps me live out my philosophy that "teachers teach students, not just content."

SUSAN BARBER *is English Department Chair at Northgate High School in Newnan, GA, where she teaches AP Literature. In addition to teaching in public schools for over 10 years, Susan has taught in private schools and even homeschooled for several years, giving her unique insight into all realms of education and learning. Having her Masters and Specialist's degrees in curriculum with a research emphasis in holistic grammar instruction, Susan believes that public education should be challenging yet accessible for students of all levels. She is an advocate for students, which is evident through her work at the county and state level on various education projects and at her blog* Teach with Class *where she writes about issues concerning the next generation. Her Twitter description says it best: "wife, mom, and caffeinated educator influencing the next generation to live worthwhile lives and love literature." Susan lives in the Atlanta area with her husband Scott, daughter Brooke, and dog Bear.*

Follow her on Twitter @susanclaireb.

Thinking Icons for Literary Analysis

Laura Bradley

"Students will learn a variety of ways to read, think about, and write analytically in response to literature. They will choose significant excerpts from text and choose lenses through which to write analytical responses to them."

PRESS THE BUTTON on the projector and my eighth graders see on the screen:

Once upon a time, there was a little girl named Goldilocks. One day she went for a walk in the forest. Pretty soon she came upon a house. She knocked, and when no one answered, she walked right in. At a table in the kitchen, there were three bowls of porridge. Goldilocks was hungry. She tasted the porridge from the first bowl.

"Mrs. Bradley," David calls out, "Why are we reading 'Goldilocks'? That's baby stuff!"

"Yeah," Sarah chimes in, "We read that in kindergarten."

"Yes, you did," I tell them, "but today you're going to read this story with new eyes. Now you are going to read like a writer. You are going to read for literary devices, and you are going to read to analyze. No longer will you read just to comprehend; now it's time to read actively." Once my students stop groaning and rolling their eyes, I point out eight icon cards that I have placed on the whiteboard.

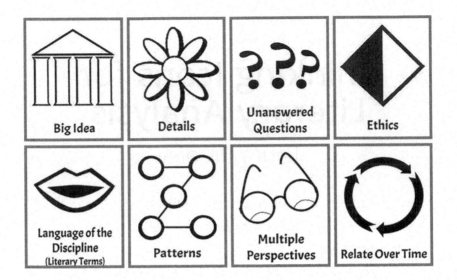

I explain that these icons represent different ways of thinking, and that they will help them learn to read analytically. Rather than defining all eight icons at once, I ask them to listen again to "Goldilocks," this time with analytical ears and eyes, and to stop me if they notice an icon that can be applied to the text.

I begin reading, "Once upon a time, there was a little girl named Goldilocks . . ." and a hand shoots up. "Yes, Sean? What do you see?"

"That's a *Pattern!*" Sean shouts, excited to be the first to connect an icon to the text.

"What do you mean? Explain the pattern."

"Well, lots of stories start out with 'Once upon a time,' so that's a pattern."

"OK, good, that is a pattern of writing. Now let's go beyond identifying the pattern. Let's think like a writer. Why does the author use this pattern? What is its purpose?" I prod Sean to move beyond the surface and into analysis.

A brief discussion follows, as students point out that children's stories use this pattern, so maybe it is a signal to the reader that a certain type of story, a fairy tale, is to follow.

"What does that mean?" I ask them. "What might a reader predict if they see this familiar pattern at the start of a story? Make a list in your notebook of what you expect from a story that starts with 'Once upon a time.' "

After they list in their notebooks for a few minutes, I ask them to share. "What can you predict from this familiar opening line?" Hands go up and students say:

"It's a fairy tale, which means it probably has a lesson for children, like don't steal or lie."

"And fairy tales have animals in them that talk, like 'Three Little Pigs' and 'Little Red Riding Hood.'"

"And magic, right? Like 'Cinderella'."

I stop them here to show them how their observations can connect to some of the icons.

I point to the *Big Idea* icon card: "When you talk about a lesson or moral of a story, like 'don't lie,' that can be a *Big Idea*, or a theme." Then I move on to the *Language of the Discipline* icon: "Also, because you noticed a pattern in the writing, you're able to predict what genre the text might be. *Genre* is part of our vocabulary of literary analysis. It's specific to English class when we are looking at categories of literature, so it's part of our *Language of the Discipline* of literary analysis. Make sense so far?" I see heads nodding as my novice analysts begin to see the many lenses through which they may read and write about literature.

I continue reading "Goldilocks" aloud, and in the first paragraph alone students identify five more icons: Jenna points to the *Unanswered Questions* icon and asks, "Why did she walk into the house?"

Tyler responds, "That's another *Unanswered Question*: How do you know it's a stranger's house? Maybe she knows them, and that's why she goes right in."

Monique offers, "I think that's going to be a *Big Idea* in the story. Wait, *Big Idea* means theme, right? 'cause I think honesty and trust

Thinking Icons for Literary Analysis
LEARNING GOALS

BROAD IMPLICATIONS

Students will understand that:

- Literary analysis can be approached through a variety of lenses.

- Analysis requires going beyond initial observations, summary or questions.

- Considering an author's intent can strengthen one's appreciation for and analysis of the text.

- Challenging texts can be made more accessible when read through the lenses of analysis.

KNOWLEDGE GAINED

Students will know:

- That not all excerpts and observations are significant enough for analysis.

- That analysis of text can include consideration of specific details, questions, and perspectives.

- That understanding an author's intent can improve one's appreciation for the text.

SKILLS ACQUIRED

Students will be able to:

- Choose significant excerpts from literature for their analysis.

- Make inferences from the text.

- Analyze text from a variety of lenses, e.g., theme, details, perspectives, unanswered questions.

EVIDENCE OF LEARNING

- As the teacher reads aloud from "Goldilocks and the Three Bears," students point out connections between the *Thinking Icons* and the text.

- In their notebooks, students list examples from an observation and share aloud.

- Students continue annotating the story on their own.

- Students compare their annotations with their partner's, discussing where their icons differ.

- As a whole class, students share out some of their annotations from the rest of the story.

- Students annotate the first chapter of John Steinbeck's *The Pearl* with *Thinking Icons*. (They will start this work in class; finish for homework).

- The next class day, students will share and discuss their annotations.

LEARNING PLAN

- Start class by reading aloud from "Goldilocks and the Three Bears," which is projected on the whiteboard so that students can follow along.

- Point out the *Thinking Icons*, which are displayed on the whiteboard, and explain that they offer a variety of ways for students to think about what they are reading. Tell the students to look for ways to apply the icons to the story as it is read aloud.

LAURA BRADLEY

- As the students call out connections between the icons and the text, ask them to explain or defend their observations, thus showing them that analysis needs to go beyond their initial observations.

- At some point in the discussion, have students list details from an observation in their notebooks. This might be a list of characteristics of a genre, of unanswered questions, of meanings behind a metaphor, etc. The students' observations help the teacher to determine what they should list in their notebooks.

- Students will share from their lists, and the teacher connects what they say to some of the other icons. At this point, explain how the variety of observations make it possible for them all to write about the same excerpt from a text, yet approach the analysis through different lenses (icons).

- After practicing together for a few paragraphs, distribute copies of the story to the students so that they can continue reading and marking icons on the text themselves.

- Circulate as they work, offering suggestions to students who aren't marking very many icons. Also challenge students to find as many different icons as they can, as students will often mark icons they find easier while avoiding others.

- Have students compare their annotations with a partner, noticing how one person may approach the text through a different icon than another.

- Allow students to share what they and their partners noticed; continue asking students to explain their comments, answer their questions, and go beyond initial observations.

- Distribute copies of chapter one of John Steinbeck's *The Pearl*, and repeat the earlier steps: read aloud while students mark icons on the text. Pause after a couple of paragraphs and asks students to share what they marked and why.

- Again modeling how analysis has to go deeper than an observation, ask students what they think the significance of a particular observation is, for instance:

  - *Why did the author include certain details? What can you infer from the details? Why might they matter?*

  - *Why did the author create a certain metaphor? How does it contribute to your understanding of the story?*

  - *What questions do you have so far about the story? What do you think the answers might be?*

  - *What is the point of view of the story? What if the story was told from a different point of view? How do you think it would be different?*

- Students continue annotating the text with icons for homework, in preparation for sharing the next day and learning to write a paragraph of analysis in response to an excerpt and icon.

LAURA BRADLEY

Handout 1

THINKING ICONS FOR LITERARY ANALYSIS

Lens for analysis:	Icon:	Key questions: (to analyze: see **bolded text** and **explain your thinking**)	Examples:
Language of the Discipline: literary analysis		What vocabulary terms are specific to literary analysis? What do you notice about these aspects of the text? **How are they significant to the story?**	character, protagonist, antagonist, plot, conflict, resolution, figurative language, simile, metaphor, personification, imagery, theme, point of view, setting, etc.
Details		What details do you notice and why do they matter? **Why has the author included those details? How are they significant to the story?**	• setting details • characterization • images
Patterns		What elements reoccur? What is the sequence or order of events? **What predictions can you make based on a pattern? Why is that pattern significant to the story?**	• time lines • predictability • repeated elements
Unanswered Questions		What information is unclear, missing, or still not known by the reader? **Why do you think the author has left it out? Try to answer the question(s), and explain why.**	• missing parts • incomplete ideas • ambiguity • discrepancies • unresolved issues
Ethics		What ethical principles do you see in the text? What is "right" or "wrong" in the situation? **Why do you think characters behave as they do? Is there an easy, right/wrong answer, or is it more complex? What is the author's purpose in including these issues?**	• values • morals • ethics • pro and con • bias • differing opinions • right and wrong • shades of gray
Big Ideas		What are the main themes in the text? How does the author communicate them? **What is the significance of the themes to the story? to the characters? to you?**	• themes • lessons • main ideas • generalizations
Relate Over Time		How are elements related in terms of the past, present, and future? **What connections do you see in the text between time periods?**	• connecting points in time • relationships within a time period
Multiple Perspectives (Points of View)		What are the opposing viewpoints? How do different characters or readers see this event or situation? **How does the point of view affect how the story is told and what the readers see?**	• different roles and knowledge • opposing viewpoints • debate

WHAT MADE IT **MEMORABLE**

Since the *Thinking Icons* help students choose deeper and more complex aspects of the literature to analyze, as well as giving them a variety of approaches to analysis, their written analysis improves dramatically over the course of the school year. I have always resisted telling my students what to write about (or giving them questions to answer) in response to literature because I want them to read actively, to learn to notice what is going on in the text, to question and think about what they read without my prompting. They need to own their analysis, to choose something from the text that resonates with them, rather than writing about what a teacher thinks is important. In my earlier attempts to teach literary analysis, I would give my students the freedom to choose what to write about from the text, but they struggled to select something specific or significant enough for quality analysis. The icons give them a variety of choices while also helping them focus on worthwhile elements of the text.

Another benefit of the icons is that they can greatly improve our class discussions about literature. If students have annotated a chapter for homework in preparation for a discussion, then they will have a variety of ways to contribute to the discussion the next day. Even reluctant students who struggle to participate in discussions can be prompted by the icons: I ask them to share aloud a quotation from the text and which icon they marked next to it, and then I encourage the students to explain why they made that connection and how they respond to it. Since no two students will have annotated the text in the same way, they are curious to hear how their peers have responded, making our discussions unpredictable and interesting.

The icons are not limited to literary analysis; they are intended to be used across all disciplines, helping students make connections from one subject to another. A social studies teacher at my school uses the icons to help his students make a variety of connections to history, especially showing them the relevance between the events of long ago and their lives today. My students tell me that they are now finding *Patterns*, *Big Ideas*, *Unanswered Questions*, and *Ethics* in their science class studies. I also have my students use the icons to annotate non-fiction pieces, which makes our discussions about texts much richer. My students learn to approach a variety of texts with an analytical eye, and that helps them tackle difficult nonfiction.

Literary analysis is one of the most challenging tasks expected of eighth graders, and it is nearly impossible if students don't have strategies for how to begin the process. Before I taught my students to use these icons, if I asked what they thought about something they had read, many would shrug their shoulders and offer up the dreaded, "I dunno." Thanks to the *Thinking Icons*, my students experiment with a variety of lenses through which to be active, analytical readers and discover their own voices as they write analytically in response.

LAURA BRADLEY *has been teaching middle school English language arts since 1988, and currently teaches English, digital design, and broadcast media at Kenilworth Junior High in Petaluma, California. She is a National Board Certified Teacher, a Google for Education Certified Innovator, a Bay Area Writing Project Teacher Consultant, and a community facilitator for Edutopia, the George Lucas Educational Foundation. She holds an MA in Education (Curriculum, Teaching and Learning: Educational Technology) and is a first place winner of the Henry Ford's Innovation Nation Teacher Innovator Award, 2015.*

In addition to teaching eighth graders full time, Laura also provides staff development in writing, project-based learning, and

Google Apps for Education. Her husband, Doug, is also a middle school teacher, and they are proud parents of college grad Chloe, and soon-to-be-college-grad Duncan.

Follow her on Twitter @LAMBRADLEY.

LAURA BRADLEY

should reflect their struggles, strengths, and ideas—not just mirror my own. I hope this lesson outline, as well as the materials, extensions, and modifications I include, demonstrate my core beliefs about teaching and learning.

The students who read *Of Mice and Men* with me are a small group of skeptical juniors who come to my classroom usually professing to "hate" English or reading…or both. They are often struggling readers or struggling students for a variety of reasons, including language barriers, lack of academic support, or lack of interest in the literature they've been forced to read, which seems irrelevant to their lives outside of school. To these students, I introduce *Of Mice and Men* as "the story that no student I have taught has ever disliked," which fortunately has proven true year after year. This bold proclamation hooks them, and I'm careful to craft our activities and discussions to nurture curiosity and provoke engagement with the colorful characters and harsh setting of Depression-era Southern California.

I teach this lesson upon completion of the novel, but it could be modified to work throughout the story. The intent is that students have been introduced to every character and have already discussed Steinbeck's characterization choices. By the end of the novel, we have probably argued about whether we love or hate Curley's wife and whether George truly loves Lennie or simply feels an obligation to take care of him. These discussions prime them for this lesson and the resulting project.

The core of this lesson is analysis of characters, but to engage my students in critical thinking, I use images as the access point to discussing motivations, flaws, and dreams. My inspiration for this approach stems from a conference session I attended a few years ago on visual literacy. I remember feeling engaged, connected, curious, and compelled by the images used by the presenter. I also remember having an "ah-ha" moment about the way images help to teach some crucial skills like analyzing varied texts, developing strong questions, taking different perspectives, and engaging reader empathy. After that session, I committed to harnessing the power of images more often in my curriculum. This lesson was one of the first where I incorporated carefully-selected images to teach my curriculum in a new way.

When I taught this lesson for the first time, I was shocked by how my students instantly engaged with the images, noticing every detail and connecting them to the characters they had come to love or hate. As we shared our connections, students respectfully disagreed with each other, explaining why their claims were stronger and pointing to different details of the pictures to support their ideas. I watched my students analyze deeply with very little instruction or scaffolding from me. While I had only planned for the discussion to take ten minutes, I remember being amazed when the bell rang. That night, I returned home and reevaluated how images could play a central role in teaching analysis, textual support, and characterization.

Since that first iteration, I have experimented with different projects and approaches. This lesson reflects what I have learned about student voice and choice as well as the enduring power of symbols and images. Every time I teach this lesson, I cannot wait to see what my students produce. If you try it with your students, continue my learning by telling me what you learn as well!

Teaching Symbolism and Characterization in *Of Mice and Men*
LEARNING GOALS

BROAD **IMPLICATIONS**

Students will understand that:

- Analysis is a process that can be used with written and visual texts.

- Analysis must be grounded in support (details from image or quotations from text).

- Analysis is subjective. A reader/viewer analyzes through individual perspective and point of view.

- Characters can be understood more deeply by identifying symbols that represent their motivations, personality, strengths, and flaws.

KNOWLEDGE GAINED

Students will know:

- How words and symbols, both literary and visual, can represent characters.

- That analysis is a subjective process grounded in objective support.

- How characters are developed through direct and indirect techniques.

- That individual experiences influence the interpretation of characters and symbols.

SKILLS ACQUIRED

Students will be able to:

- Analyze visual text to make connections with written text.

- Support a claim with observable details.

- Read critically to find textual evidence to support characterization.

- Understand visual and literary symbols.

- Interpret the motivations and actions of a character through visual and written text.

EVIDENCE OF LEARNING

- Student observations go beyond the obvious and demonstrate ability to deconstruct images in order to analyze them.

- Student connections are supported with multiple details from both visual and written text.

- Student demonstrates a creative approach to crafting a visual symbol for a chosen character.

- Student demonstrates ability to link textual evidence to a claim.

- Student discussions enhance understanding of both symbolism and characterization.

LEARNING PLAN

DAY ONE

- As the teacher displays three images, students will list observations about each image.

student leadership, mastery of established goals, and student understandings.

- Students conclude the discussion by reflecting on ways their understanding of the characters and images was deepened by listening to the perspectives and interpretations of their peers.

- The teacher shares observations made during the discussion and clarifies any misunderstandings, pointing to examples of student analysis as models for the class.

DAY TWO/THREE

- Students receive a project description that explains their task. (See **Handout 3**.)

- Students independently choose a character of focus and brainstorm that character's most significant flaw and American dream based on characterization in the novel *Of Mice and Men*.

- After their brainstorm, students choose which aspect of their character they want to depict visually: the flaw or the dream.

- Students then either draw, paint, or collage symbols (from magazines or other media) to create their visual representation of this character, incorporating two passages of text.

- Students present or publish their projects with either a written or verbal explanation of their images, explaining the connections among the visual symbols, the character analysis, and the textual evidence.

Extensions, Technology Modifications, Learning Modifications

- Rather than using teacher-selected images for the second practice, students could conduct a *Google* search to find images that represent a character in the text. This lesson could incorporate quality search queries, creative commons attribution, and other digital literacy skills.

- Students could create and present their project and analyses using iPad or mobile apps that allow for image annotation or audio embedding. Some examples of these are *Skitch*, *Notability*, *VoiceThread*, and *Adobe Voice*. Some examples of web tools that could serve this purpose are *Checkthis*, *Piktochart*, *Canva*, and *Google Slides*.

- To scaffold younger students or students who need more support, the teacher could model using textual passages to support each of the three images in the first series, conducting a "think aloud" to make connections and the process of analysis transparent.

- Students could work on the project collaboratively in pairs to depict one character's flaw and dream, using images to support both.

- Students could conduct a compare/contrast reflection that asks them to reflect on how a different person or group depicted the same character and what they learned from that student's project.

- Students could create an image that symbolizes some aspect of their own personality, dream, flaw, or strength.

- For a more kinesthetic approach in the final project, organize a school scavenger hunt where students use their mobile devices (or borrowed school devices) to take pictures of objects or scenes that could symbolize their chosen character as the class walks through the school. The final product is the same, but class time is given for the picture hunt.

BRIANNA CROWLEY

HANDOUTS/RESOURCES

Handout 1

Handout 2

Name	Period/Class	OMAM Characterization and Symbolism Handout

1
Observations:

2
Observations:

3
Observations:

Handout 3

1 Character	**2** Character
Reasons linked to observations (min. 3)	Reasons linked to observations (min. 3)
Textual Evidence (include parenthetical citation)	Textual Evidence (include parenthetical citation)

Candy

Curley's Wife

Curley

Crooks

3 Character	**4** Character
Reasons linked to observations (min. 3)	Reasons linked to observations (min. 3)
Textual Evidence (include parenthetical citation)	Textual Evidence (include parenthetical citation)

BRIANNA CROWLEY

Handout 4

You don't understand. And I can't explain.

Handout 5

Name   OMAM Symbolism Project   Period   Date

Symbolism Project: Defining the Characters

A symbol is a tangible object or action that represents something else. After finishing *Of Mice and Men*, you have learned a great deal about each of the character's personalities. In this assignment, you will demonstrate your understanding of one character through the use of **symbolism**.

Step 1: What character in *Of Mice and Men* intrigues (interests) you? Identify this character and explain why on the lines below. Please use complete sentences.

_____

_____

_____

_____

Step 2: Think about this character's personality and behaviors. What do you think are the most important traits of this character? List them below.

-
-
-
-

Step 3: What is this character's fatal flaw or dream? Brainstorm below.

Flaw	Dream

WHAT MADE IT **MEMORABLE**

Students never cease to amaze me. When presented with simple images, they bring a deep range of perspectives and interpretations. While some saw the single bird on the wire as George in his isolation from the other ranch hands because of Lennie, other students saw that same bird as symbolic of Curley — isolated because of anger and insecurity. As students presented their analysis, I felt a nearly tangible expansion in the room. Each of us expanded our personal understanding to include new perspectives.

This lesson became a bonding moment for my class as they discussed characters as complex humans with hidden motivations and glaring fallibilities. Some students viewed unlovable characters through a lens of empathy, perhaps relating to the character's behavior or perceived needs. These students helped the rest of us consider characters, and perhaps even each other, in a new light.

Yes, I covered important standards, and yes, I enjoyed seeing my students support their ideas with text. But what I love about this lesson is the spark of curiosity in students' eyes as the images are unveiled, and the burst of creativity unleashed as students create symbols for their chosen characters. This lesson makes literature and my classroom come alive, and that's why I'll continue to teach, modify, and share it year after year.

BRIANNA CROWLEY *opened her classroom doors in autumn 2015 on her ninth year of teaching high school English in the sweetest town on earth: Hershey, Pennsylvania. In addition to this role, she also serves as an Instructional Technology Coach, helping her colleagues leverage technology in their classrooms. Brianna recently completed a year serving in a hybrid role as a Teacherpreneur with The*

Center for Teaching Quality. In that unique role, she helped teacher leaders across the U.S. become more effective communicators and advocates for their students and the profession. In 2014, she was named a PA Keystone STAR educator and also served in ASCD's 2013 class of Emerging Leaders. When not scrolling her Twitter feed for inspiration or attending a poetry slam, Brianna likes to tackle home improvement projects, improve her 5K run time, and enjoy the newest restaurant in town.

Brianna is usually reading four books and listening to a fifth. She has lived in three countries, travelled to nearly a dozen more, but is always on the lookout for new experiences around the corner.

Follow her on Twitter @AkaMsCrowley.

Ignite Talks

Gerard Dawson

"We grow when we are pushed to the edges of our capabilities. When students perform, hit 'publish,' and put themselves out there in their own way, real learning happens."

THERE'S A SAFETY that comes with the literary essay. Students receive the assignment, complete it, hand it in, and get a grade. Follow a formula and there is little risk for the teacher, little risk for the student. But as my long-time mentor, Bill Sowder, would say, "When does a structure become a crutch? When does a routine become a rut?"

When it comes to my own teaching, I sometimes find my routines turning into ruts: the same lessons, the same assignments, again and again. Last year, I decided to do something different.

On the first day of school, before reviewing the syllabus or doing ice breakers, I recited a poem — "Introduction to Poetry" by Billy Collins — from memory for my students. My stomach filled with butterflies as each student entered and the class quieted down to hear the poem. I recited it for each class with a few stumbles. The students reacted subtly, yet they seemed pleased to have a break from the typical first day activities.

This set the groundwork for a year-long theme, a way of taking risks in learning that required students and me to "put ourselves out there." If we wrote, we shared it with readers outside of the classroom.

If we held a discussion, we recorded it, played it back, and listened to feedback. If we researched, we emailed experts in the field to get closer to the source.

The motivation behind this theme of "putting ourselves out there" was to stop both the teacher and the student from "playing school." A fear of mine is that students feel that they are doing "school" just for a grade, and by constantly reminding myself of this year-long theme, I kept motivated to remove those inauthentic assignments and replace them with more meaningful ones.

The best example of this theme occurred towards the middle of the year, when students delivered Ignite Talks. If you have ever given an Ignite Talk, then you know it involves putting yourself on display in a big way. This style of presentation turns the typical slideshow on its head. Ignite Talks:

- Last five minutes.

- Contain 20 slides, which auto-advance every 15 seconds.

- Are delivered without a script or notes.

- Rely on image slides, not "sea of text" slides.

- Make a succinct argument.

These talks served as the summative assessment for our "Nature and Literature" unit. Throughout the unit, we explored three essential questions:

1. *How do humans view our relationship to nature?*

2. *How does nature act as a force in literature and our lives?*

3. *How can we resolve conflicts between humanity and nature?*

Students read from a small list of novels, including *Lord of the Flies*, *The Things They Carried*, *My Antonia*, and *Things Fall Apart*. We held weekly discussion groups where students shared their own questions about the novels. Adhering to the theme of putting ourselves out there, sometimes students recorded the discussions and played them back for each other or sent them to me for review.

On the days leading up to the Ignite Talks, the tone of the class grew serious. There was focus, little shirking of responsibilities, and lots of practice.

To kick off presentation day, I delivered my own Ignite Talk, on an environmental topic I had found interesting and researched. It seemed appropriate to our year-long mandate for the teacher to have the same experience that students would have.

The students gave their presentations: some soared, and to be honest, some flopped. All learned a lot, and everyone left their comfort zones.

* Thank you to my colleague Joe Petrucelli for collaborating with me on this.

Ignite Talks
LEARNING GOALS

BROAD **IMPLICATIONS**

Students will understand that:

- Literature reveals insights into modern life.

- An engaging speech requires planning, preparation, and practice.

- Humans are inextricably linked to the environment.

KNOWLEDGE GAINED

Students will know:

- The difference between factual, inductive, and analytical questions.

- The details of a self-selected environmental issue.

- The characteristics of an engaging speech.

SKILLS ACQUIRED

Students will be able to:

- Ask and answer challenging questions.

- Convey an argument using anecdotes, facts, and other evidence.

- Synthesize information from multiple sources.

- Take a position on an issue.

- Use images in a concrete and abstract way to support a message.

EVIDENCE OF LEARNING

- Weekly small group book discussions. (The teacher listens in or has the students record themselves.)

- Student-generated reading questions and written responses.

- Whole class discussions of unit essential questions.

- Discussion of sample Ignite Talks.

- Student Ignite Talks.

LEARNING PLAN

Preparation

Students read from a small list of novels, including: *Lord of the Flies*, *The Things They Carried*, *My Antonia*, and *Things Fall Apart*. They hold weekly small group discussions, focusing on their own self-created questions and the unit topic of "Nature and Literature."

DAY 1

- As students finish reading their novels, have the class conduct a "research rally." This requires access to computers or smartphones. Give students a set amount of time (we used about 40 minutes) to research and collect as many current examples of environmental issues as they can. You might provide themes or essential questions to focus students.

- Review the issues that students find and then ask student groups to select issues that are interesting and relevant to their novels.

GERARD DAWSON

DAY 2

- Introduce the Ignite Talk to students by showing them "How and Why to Give an Ignite Talk" by Scott Berkun. (https://www.youtube.com/watch?v=yGENcskRGRk)

- Throughout the next few days, watch a different Ignite Talk daily and discuss the qualities of a successful talk.

- Discuss these questions with students:

  - *"How does this type of presentation differ from typical school presentations?"*

  - *"How would you feel about delivering this type of presentation?"*

- Review the assignment requirements and rubric with students. (See **Handout 1 and Handout 2.**)

- Students discuss their presentation plans. Conduct conferences with student groups.

DAYS 3-5

- Groups complete these steps at their own pace as the teacher confers with the groups:

  - Select excerpts from the novels related to unit essential questions.

  - Research environmental issues related to the essential questions.

  - Outline the presentation using a blank slide template.

  - Find images to use for the slides (remember: little to no text is used on slides during an Ignite Talk).

  - Practice!

DAY 6

- Students present their Ignite Talks.

- During the talks, every student writes a one-sentence summary of each group's argument.

- Students reflect on their presentation experience by answering:

  - *"What did you learn from this experience?"*

  - *"How should the teacher change this experience for future classes?"*

HANDOUTS/RESOURCES

Teacher resources:

- *What's the Big Idea?* by Jim Burke

- *Crafting Digital Writing* by Troy Hicks

- "Teaching Presentation Skills with Ignite" by Andrew Miller, *Edutopia*

- "How and Why to Give an Ignite Talk" by Scott Berkun (https://www.youtube.com/watch?v=yGENcskRGRk)

- "The Illusion of Speed" by Steve Souders (https://www.youtube.com/watch?v=bGYgFYG2Ccw)

Novels:

- *Lord of the Flies* by William Golding

- *My Antonia* by Willa Cather

- *The Things They Carried* by Tim O'Brien

- *Things Fall Apart* by Chinua Achebe

GERARD DAWSON

Handout 1

IGNITE TALK ASSIGNMENT SHEET

Unit Essential Questions:

1. How do humans view our relationship to nature?

2. How does nature act as a force in literature and/or our lives?

3. How can we resolve conflicts between humanity and nature?

What's the assignment? Present an Ignite Talk that answers one of our unit's essential questions.

You're required to use at least two sources when researching and preparing your talk. One must be a source about a current environmental issue. The other *can* be your novel, though it doesn't have to be. It can also be another outside source.

What is an Ignite Presentation?

Ignite is a presentation format used at conferences around the country. Format of the presentation:

- Five minutes long

- Contains twenty slides

- Each slide is shown for 15 seconds (15 seconds X 20 slides = 5 minutes)

- Images only on the slides

- No script used by the speaker(s)

This project requires you to...

- Convey an argument using engaging anecdotes, examples, facts and statistics.

- Synthesize information from a variety of sources into an original idea.

- Take a clear position on a question.

- Speak smoothly and confidently in front of a crowd (without a script).

- Use images in a concrete and abstract way to support your message.

Here's the process we'll follow:

1. Research. Read. Discuss with your group. Determine an answer to your essential question and the environmental issue or parts of your book you'll use to prove your argument.

2. Create an outline. The format is up to you (traditional, web, chart, infographic), but you must submit a physical product. The outline should include 3-5 big ideas you want to share and the anecdotes, examples, facts, statistics, or arguments you'll use to support these ideas.

3. Use *Google* Slides to collaboratively compose the script, spread across the 20 slides. It will look like this.

4. Get rid of the text (save it on a document), and turn each slide into an image that describes or represents the idea of the slide.

5. Practice, practice, practice.

6. Practice again.

7. Present!

GERARD DAWSON

Handout 2
IGNITE PRESENTATION RUBRIC

	Exceeds Standard (A)	Meets Standard (B-C)	Approaches Standard (D-F)
Argument & Ideas	You connected anecdotes, examples, and statistics seamlessly to develop your unique answer to the essential question.	You developed an argument using valid reasoning and relevant and sufficient evidence.	You made an observation instead of an argument or provided insufficient or incomplete evidence for your argument.
Speaking	You were poised, prepared and well-paced. You spoke smoothly throughout, and were able to recover smoothly from any slip-ups. You were enthusiastic, professional, and kept the audience engaged throughout the presentation.	You spoke clearly, concisely, and logically, so that the audience could follow your argument. Your style and delivery were appropriate for your purpose, audience, and task.	You completed the presentation and followed the format, but could've used more preparation and practice.
Slides	You used images both concretely and abstractly to elevate your argument to a new level of impact.	You used images well to enhance your arguments and add interest.	The images depicted exactly what you talked about in a concrete way throughout, or they may have been distracting or confusing.

WHAT MADE IT **MEMORABLE**

I sat in the back of the classroom, watching one "quiet" student engage his peers with an entertaining, informative talk. He had prepared and practiced, and his few minutes were a cut above the rest. The whole class, including me, was a bit surprised at his natural speaking ability. As the class applauded, and the bell rang, I came to a realization: *How often do I leave student talents unappreciated?*

After this unit, I made room for students to share their talents in their own ways. Carly performed original songs on guitar and vocals, Ravali wrote and illustrated a hilarious graphic novel, others performed skits or recorded short films.

Early in my career I struggled to have students demonstrate their learning in authentic and engaging ways. With writing I can easily have students create products similar to those that they read in the real world. They can write an editorial, a blog post, or an online portfolio. But I've always struggled to keep my literature instruction feeling fresh in the same way.

This project marked a shift in my teaching of reading, as I realized that creative assessments are not only the domain of my writing instruction.

Unlike a typical presentation day in class, where students (and teachers) may feel bored, these were exciting class periods. I'd like to invite other teachers, administrators, and even parents and community members to watch future Ignite Talks.

In the future I would include even more time for practice and feedback. Students could deliver their talk to another small group of students, get honest feedback, then hone their slideshow or presentation in order to be more engaging, informative, and concise. This would mimic the feedback loop that I value in the writing process.

During end-of-the-year surveys, many students said that the Ignite Talk was both the most challenging and most valuable activity that we did during the year. Little did they know their teacher learned a lot more from the experience than they did.

GERARD DAWSON

GERARD DAWSON *teaches English and journalism at Hightstown High School in New Jersey. He is motivated by collaborating with colleagues and leveraging technology to discover new teaching practices. He writes about literacy and technology on his blog, www.GerardDawson. org. Gerard lives in New Jersey with his wife, Jennifer, and son, Gerard.*

Follow him on Twitter @GerardDawson3

Multi-Draft Reading Using Print and Visual Texts

Todd Finley

"My main goal is to help students realize that deeper analytical reading of print and visual texts can be achieved through re-reading. I also want students to see how inquiry can be aided when both a "paradigmatic" and "narrative" lens are used. More important than the literature and visual texts chosen are the analytical skills that can be transferred to subsequent texts."

IN THE EARLY 1990s I took a trip away from snowbound Minneapolis where I taught 7-12th grade English to attend a regional conference. During a memorable session on reader response that was facilitated by Robert Probst — the prolific author and silver-haired guru of literature pedagogy — I read and discussed a short story with a small group of English teachers. The activity was deceptively simple: we read, re-read, wrote, and discussed a short story, and made text-to-self, text-to-text, and text-to-world connections.

To my surprise, Probst didn't hold forth, despite his stature in the profession. He hung back, watching, smiling, and trusting in the power of the short story and our discussions to make the event meaningful.

In other words, *he let the activity breathe.* By the end of the conference session, all the participants felt profoundly connected to each other and to the literature.

From that experience with Bob Probst, I learned new principles of teaching literature that I use to this day:

- *Principle 1: Reading is a multi-draft process.* Similarly to how writers deepen their thinking each time they compose a draft, readers add substantially to their understanding each time they re-read a text.

- *Principle 2: Provide ample processing time for small group discussion of a text.* Give students enough space to lose themselves in the great mysteries of literature and then orient themselves with the help of peers.

- *Principle 3: Don't teach the life out of a text.* The primary utility of literature is not the identification and analysis of literary features. Overemphasis on content knowledge and skills can kill an opportunity to help students connect their life stories with literature.

Over the years, experience has taught me another trick. Before having students analyze literature, I have them first learn and apply analytical skills with visual texts: photos, paintings, movies, infographics, etc. Visual literacy processes can be easier for students, particularly given that 75% of all information processing neurons receive visual information. Once they have internalized a process using visual texts, I know they're ready to do the same with print texts.

The richest application of the aforementioned principles is embedded in the following lesson for 7-12th graders. Depending on which texts are selected, the activities can be shortened to a single period or implemented over three hours. Although the lesson uses the texts pasted below this paragraph, it will work equally well if you substitute my choices with your preferred visual and print texts.

Texts Used for this Lesson	Where the Texts Can be Located Online
"A Dead Body" by Anton Chekhov	http://bit.ly/ChekhovTBF
Winter, 1946 by Andrew Wyeth	http://bit.ly/WyethTBF (Click on the image of a boy running down a hill)
Juanita's Bodega by Joan Steiner	http://bit.ly/BodegaTBF

Multi-Draft Reading Using Print and Visual Texts
LEARNING GOALS

BROAD **IMPLICATIONS**
Students will understand that:

- A multi-draft strategy — typically associated with composing — can deepen students' engagement and interpretations.

- There are two primary ways of *knowing*: Paradigmatic versus Narrative Knowing (Jerome Bruner).

KNOWLEDGE GAINED
Students will know:

- How to identify practices associated with paradigmatic and narrative modes of inquiry ("ways of knowing").

- How to define *inference*.

- How to use similes to interpret a text.

SKILLS ACQUIRED
Students will be able to:

- Use reading, writing, speaking, listening, and visualizing to make inferences.

- Practice inquiry strategies that can be applied across content areas.

- Make text-to-self, text-to-text, and text-to-world connections (Zimmerman, 1997).

- Engage in multi-draft observing: doodling, observing, and adding detail.

- Engage in critical thinking and perspective taking.

EVIDENCE OF LEARNING

- Students will participate in a multi-draft viewing exercise during a whole group discussion of Joan Steiner's painting, *Juanita's Bodega*. After showing the image for 15 seconds, the instructor will ask, "What did you see? What else did you see? What else?"

- Students will engage in a multi-draft comprehension of "A Dead Body" by focusing on three different elements of the short story as they read and re-read the text, noting important moments, new discoveries, and unanswered questions. Those three topics will be discussed in small groups.

- In order to engage in visual literacy and take part in a multi-draft observing process, students will complete an exercise involving close looking and sketching of *Winter, 1946,* a painting by Andrew Wyeth.

- Students will make text-to-text and text-to-world connections related to "A Dead Body."

- As a way to interpret "A Dead Body," students will write 10 similes about the short story and then follow a protocol to rework the simile list as a poem.

- As a closing activity, students will write three things they learned, two things that left them wondering, and one thing that they want the instructor to know.

TODD FINLEY

LEARNING PLAN

- Introduction – Explain that the class is about to analyze visual and print texts using a process called "multi-draft" reading and viewing. Ask if any of the students might hazard a guess as to what that might mean.

- Tell the students that multi-draft reading/viewing involves making inferences. Write the following definition of *inference* on the chalkboard or whiteboard: "An inference is a judgment based on reasoning rather than on a direct statement in a text. It is a critical element of inquiry (investigating and seeking information by asking questions)."

- Multi-Draft Viewing:

  - Project an image of Joan Steiner's *Juanita's Bodega* (*http*://bit.ly/BodegaTBF). After 15 seconds, transition to a blank screen. Ask students: "What did you see? What else did you see? What else?"

  - Again, project an image of Joan Steiner's *Juanita's Bodega. After* 15 seconds, transition to a blank screen. Ask students: "What did you see? What else did you see? What else?"

  - Finally, project an image of Joan Steiner's *Juanita's Bodega and* keep the artwork on the screen. Ask students: "What else do you see that you didn't identify before? What else? What else?"

  - Ask: "What helped you identify new things in the text?" (Answers might include *getting a chance to observe multiple times* and *listening to peers' responses*.)

- Multi-Draft Reading

  - Distribute a handout of "A Dead Body" by Anton Chekhov (http://bit.ly/ChekhovTBF). Tell students that they will be reading this text three times, paying attention to different features of the text during each iteration.

  - 1st Read: Underline important moments. Discuss your findings with a small group for 10 minutes.

  - 2nd Read: Mark new discoveries. Discuss your findings with a small group for 8 minutes.

  - 3rd Read: Write down what questions are still unanswered. Discuss your findings with a small group for 10 minutes.

  - Ask students to discuss if they learned new things about the text through the re-reading and discussion process. Also mention that in the same way that multiple drafts lead to deeper understanding of a subject by a writer, multiple reading leads to deeper understanding by a reader.

  - Provide a quick overview of two modes of knowing that occur during the inquiry process: Jerome Bruner's *Paradigmatic* versus *Narrative Knowing* (See **Handout 1** at the end of this lesson). Explain that during the next few exercises, students will be engaging in an interpretation exercise using both modes.

  - Observing as a Multi-Draft Process: Close Looking/ Sketching

  - Explain to students that they will be observing and sketching a painting called *Winter, 1946* by Andrew Newell Wyeth. They will need a blank piece of paper

and a pencil, but should not sketch or make any notes
until they receive instructions to do so.

- Project the image of *Winter, 1946* (http://bit.ly/Wyeth_
TBF) without giving any more context about the
painting. Ask students to carefully observe the details
of the painting. After 1 minute, stop projecting the
image. Instruct the students as follows: "For 2 minutes, sketch what you remember about the image in the
space below without looking at the work of art."

- Ask students to put their pencils down. Then project
the image again for 1 minute. Have students study the
image closely for details that they might have missed.
Stop projecting the image and ask students to add or
subtract details from their sketches for 1 minute.

- Project the painting one more time, and leave it on
screen. Shift the students into small groups to share what
they drew. Have them discuss what they noticed at the
end of the observing and drawing exercises that they
didn't notice during their first observation. (*Optional:*
During this part of the lesson, I usually take a picture of
each drawing with my smart phone and email the images
to my *Evernote* account — a cloud-based storage and note
taking service. Later, I project these images for the entire
class to see the variety of representations. At this point,
I can also have students discuss the key features of the
visual text that were emphasized in the drawings.)

- In the next phase, ask the small student teams to make
text-to-self connections (finding connections between
the text and something in their own experience) for
about 8 minutes by answering these questions: "Does
anything in the work of art remind you of something

in your own life? How so? How well do you relate to 'A Dead Body' by Chekhov? Explain."

- In the next phase, ask the small student teams to make text-to-text connections (finding connections between the work of art and another text) for about 15 minutes. Distribute "All About Andrew Wyeth's *Winter, 1946*" (See **Handout 2**) and read it aloud to the class. Then have students answer these questions in small groups:

- How does the new information change the way you view the painting?

- How is the painting similar to "A Dead Body" by Anton Chekhov, given the additional written context about the piece?

- How is this painting different from "A Dead Body" by Anton Chekhov, given the additional written context about the piece?

- As individuals, have students write similes about the work by completing a handout (See **Handout 3**) with 10 simile statements: "'A Dead Body' by Chekhov is like _____." After learners have filled in all the blanks, have them...

- Delete the least resonant line.

- Combine two lines and make them into one.

- Title the poem, "I am.... "

- Remove any lines that don't fit.

- As the final step, replace all "'*A Dead Body*' by Chekhov is like" phrases with "*I am*" and cross out any lines that don't fit the new context (describing the student, not the short story).

- Invite students to read their poems aloud.

- Closing Activity: 3-2-1. Have students write the following on scratch paper to turn into the instructor.

TODD FINLEY

- 3 things you learned.

- 2 things that left you wondering.

- 1 thing that you want the instructor to know.

HANDOUTS/RESOURCES

Handout 1

JEROME BRUNER'S TWO TYPES OF KNOWING

(Both are ways of representing and interpreting reality)

Narrative Knowing	Paradigmatic Knowing
The imaginative application of the **narrative** mode leads to good stories, gripping drama, believable (though not necessarily "true") historical accounts. It deals in human or human-like intention and action and the vicissitudes and consequences that mark their course. It strives to put its timeless miracles into the particulars of experience, and to locate the experience in time and place. Joyce thought of the particularities of the story as epiphanies of the ordinary.	The logical-scientific mode attempts to fulfill the ideal of a formal, mathematical system of description and explanation. It employs categorization or conceptualization and the operations by which categories are established, instantiated, idealized, and related one to the other to form a system ....
Narrative Knowing Includes... • Stories • Metaphor • Situations • Context	Paradigmatic Knowing Includes... • Taxonomies • Abstractions • Principles

Handout 2

"All About Andrew Wyeth's *Winter, 1946*"

The most literal expression of grief in Wyeth's work is his 1946 painting *Winter, 1946*, which depicts a lone boy running by the road of a barren hillside – the same road where Wyeth's father died in a car crash. There's a simultaneous sense of movement and paralyzation in the boy's movement – exactly the sensation we feel when a loved one dies. The landscape shares the same color palette, the same grief, as its inhabitant. "I prefer winter and fall," said Wyeth, "[it's] when you feel the bone structure of the landscape — the loneliness of it, the dead feeling of winter. Something waits beneath it. The whole story doesn't show."

That's why Wyeth's work can't be reduced to quaint dabbles in realist landscapes. There's something profound beneath every brush-stroke. We can't see the whole story – but we can feel it.

- See more at this link: http://blog.sevenponds.com.

Handout 3

SIMILE POEM

Write at least 10 simile statements about "A Dead Body" by Anton Chekhov by completing the following statements:

"A Dead Body" by Chekhov is like _____
_____.

"A Dead Body" by Chekhov is like _____
_____.

"A Dead Body" by Chekhov is like _____
_____.

"A Dead Body" by Chekhov is like _____
_____.

"A Dead Body" by Chekhov is like _____
_____.

"A Dead Body" by Chekhov is like _____
_____.

"A Dead Body" by Chekhov is like _____
_____.

"A Dead Body" by Chekhov is like _____
_____.

"A Dead Body" by Chekhov is like _____
_____.

"A Dead Body" by Chekhov is like _____
_____.

TODD FINLEY

WHAT MADE IT **MEMORABLE**

I know when I've developed a good lesson plan by the feeling I get in my gut right before class starts — a feeling that all the elements of the lesson have been carefully thought through and that success is likely as long as I pay attention to students' cues.

Why is the lesson described above successful? Because I can say yes to all of the following questions in relation to the lesson:

- Does the lesson involve minimal teacher talk?

- Does the lesson have students reading, writing, speaking, listening, and viewing?

- Is there an obvious alignment with standards for my discipline?

- Are there a variety of activities that extend understanding/ use of core skills and concepts?

- Are there opportunities for critical thinking (both independently and in a small groups)?

- Have all the possible cul-de-sacs been removed? Is the lesson efficient?

- Is there more than one right answer?

- Does the lesson help students understand or shape their identities?

- Is there an element of surprise as connections are made?

- Does the lesson engage students' emotions?

- Is there constructivist pedagogy at work?

- Does the lesson involve inquiry?

A few months ago, an 18-year-old I'll call "Mary" came to the part of the lesson where her simile poem switched scaffolding from *"A Dead*

Body' by Chekhov is like" to *"I am..."* (except that we were using a Salvador Dali painting for analysis; as mentioned earlier, the lesson still works when you swap out different print and visual texts). Looking at her poem, she pulled away from her paper in surprise and said, "This is me!" When I asked her what she meant by that, she explained that she'd been experiencing some doubts about her family's religion. She didn't want to part with the poem, so I took a photo of it with my smartphone, typed it up, and pasted it below (used by permission):

I Am

I am mean velvet.
I am a fake chime.
I am the painting clinging.
I am a grinning Christmas.
I am chipped nail polish tearing.
I am the pop of an exclamation point.
I am a goodnight whispered.
I am plastic church bells.

Year after year, students report that their experiences with this lesson deepened their understanding of both visual and literary texts. They also say that the protocols helped them see how reading a text thoughtfully means perseverance and re-reading. More importantly, it's a lesson that gets remembered — a sure fire way to tell that concepts and skills have been successfully internalized.

It's not unusual to develop a strong bond with a quality lesson. Like a long-term friendship, the lesson grows in power as you thoughtfully engage with it. Multi-Draft Reading Using Print and Visual Texts is that dependable friend.

TODD BLAKE FINLEY, *PhD, is a tenured professor of English Education at East Carolina University and a blogger and assistant editor at Edutopia (George Lucas Educational Foundation). He has taught elementary school and seventh - twelfth grade English. His books are* Dinkytown Braves *and* Rethinking Classroom Design *(Rowman & Littlefield) co-written with Blake Wiggs. His blog is Todd's Brain.*

Follow him on Twitter: @finleyt.

Student-Generated Questions Using Science Fiction

Joy Kirr

"Students' questions often go unasked and unanswered. We need to give them space to ask their own questions and find the answers together. This can be a catalyst to get students asking the questions and learning from each other for life."

IT WAS REALLY only my seventh year of teaching in a classroom, even if it was my 20th year as a teacher. Seventh grade is a different animal - the students are "old enough to know better, but still too young to care..." and we need to make sure what we share with them is engaging, as their minds are hardly ever on the lesson at hand. We have four teachers on our seventh grade ELA (English Language Arts) team who work tirelessly to engage our readers and writers.

So...we come to the ever-morphing "science fiction unit." We've wondered when in the year to teach science fiction to seventh graders (right before or right after winter break), and have struggled with which pieces of text to use. "Eighth grade gets all the best stories!" we repeat every year.

We have realized it's not always the text that students love or despise - it's the activities. We used to begin this unit by teaching students the elements of science fiction through a slideshow. I now begin with a *Kahoot!* game that helps explain the differences between science fiction and fantasy. I also incorporate three video book talks a day (see them at tinyurl.com/MSSciFiBookTrailers), as I hope students will add some of these titles to their "to read next" list. The next four days incorporate three short stories with a focus on QUESTIONING.

I am fortunate to be in a district that does not "teach to the test." Therefore, I can let the students' ideas drive much of the learning that occurs. Although we, as a team of teachers, could come up with two-tier PARCC practice questions for the stories we're using, we wanted to see what questions the students had. I know that if students develop the questions, they will be learning more than if they just answered mine. I wanted them to think like readers - asking authentic questions for stories that make you think. What better stories to start with than from science fiction? We scoured all of our resources, and we found the following stories (plus one or two more) that we thought seventh graders would enjoy. For the rest of the year, we were able to use these lessons to promote creation of inferential questions to keep discussions going and learn from each other, as readers so often do.

Student-Generated Questions Using Science Fiction
LEARNING GOALS

JOY KIRR

BROAD **IMPLICATIONS**

Students will understand that:

- Readers naturally are inquisitive and ask questions about texts they are reading.

- We ask questions to stay engaged in reading (and life) and to better understand an author's (or another person's) message.

KNOWLEDGE GAINED

Students will know:

- The three categories of questioning (literal, inferential, and critical).

- That asking and answering questions *they* create will help them better understand an author's message.

- That some of their questions just cannot be answered based on what we know from the text. (These will be questions to ponder.)

SKILLS ACQUIRED

Students will be able to:

- Generate their own questions for each category (literal, inferential, critical) while reading texts.

- Find answers to their own literal questions with the help of classmates.

- Support reasonable answers to their inferential questions using textual support.

EVIDENCE OF LEARNING

- Students will generate and record all questions they have from reading a text.

- Students will share their questions with each other and work to answer them together.

- Students will organize their questions into three types (literal, inferential, critical).

- Students will find textual support to answer classmates' inferential questions.

- Students will discuss and write in response to an inferential question using textual support.

LEARNING PLAN

FOUR-DAY LESSON PLAN:

DAY ONE

Preparation:

- Each student will need available a copy of the story "Evil Robot Monkey" by Mary Robinette Kowal. (A class set should be fine.)

- Each student will need a place to write questions about the story.

- Each table group will need a device.

- Set up a page on *Padlet* or another site (*Linoit* or *Google* Doc) where students can add and see each other's responses, and you can edit and sort them. Be sure you can project this for all students to see.

- Have the projection about the "three ways of thinking" ready to share. This resource is from Ariel Sack's book *Whole Novels for the Whole Class: A Student-centered Approach*, 2013. Note: If you do not have enough technology resources, you can do any of these activities using sticky notes and butcher paper or a whiteboard.

Plans:

- Discuss the goal of the lesson — to write as many questions as you can about this story. Make sure students have something with which to write, and on which to write.

- Discuss WHY we're writing questions. What's the point?

- Direct students to read the story one time independently, writing down their questions.

- Ask students to share their questions with their table groups, and see which ones their table peers can help them answer.

- Read the story aloud, asking students to write down more questions, and/or cross out questions that were answered from this second reading.

- Each table group gets a device, and is asked to go to a *Padlet* site and add the question(s) they consider important or interesting. Ask them to have only ONE question per entry. I tried this having individual students add questions and answers the first time, and it did NOT go well. Doing this in groups of three or four makes the *Padlet* questions much easier to manage.

- Students return the device when they're finished — this makes managing the rest of the *Padlet* easier.

- Explain the three ways of thinking listed below. I convert this to types of questions - ONE at a time.

The Three Ways of Thinking

Literal	Your Thought was stated directly in the text, like a fact from the text.
Inferential	Your thought was not stated directly, but there is evidence for it in the text; it is hinted at, suggested, or implied.
Critical	Your original thought, opinion, connection, or critical question related to the text.

- Introduce the "literal" question idea, type it on the *Padlet* on the left side, and ask students to find the questions that go under that "literal" label.

- When you introduce "inferential" and "critical," do the same.

This is how our *Padlet* looked the first day. (Notice how Austin's question was two-fold, so we put it at the very bottom.)

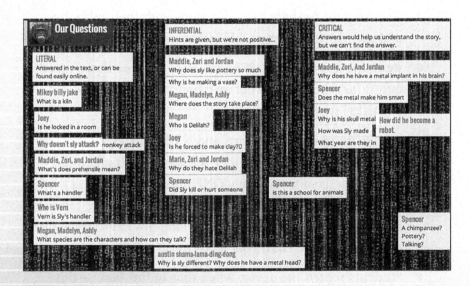

DAY TWO

Preparation:

- Each student will need available a copy of the story "Dark They Were and Golden-Eyed" by Ray Bradbury. (A class set is fine — this story is in our current textbook.)

- Each student will need a copy of the "reading check" included in the resources.

- Each student will need a place to write questions about the story.

- Each table group will need a device.

- Set up a page on *Padlet* or another site (*Linoit* or *Google* Doc) where students can add and see each other's responses, and you can edit and sort them.

Plans:

- Review WHY we are spending so much time asking questions.

- Begin reading the story — the students' job is to write questions as we read.

- After a certain page, hand out the reading check, and ask students to answer questions 1-4 in their table groups, discussing which type of question each one is.

  1. *Why does Mrs. Bittering want to stay on Mars at the beginning of the story?*

  2. *How does Harry feel when he and his family first land on Mars?*

  3. *Roses turning green, eyes turning yellow, and cows growing an extra horn all contribute to creating a(n) _____ mood.*

4. *What prevents the Bittering family from returning to Earth?*

- Share with the class which questions are literal, inferential, and critical. Move those questions under the correct heading on the new *Padlet* you created.

- After the entire story is finished, ask students to share their questions about the story at their tables, and get answers from peers to some issues they do not understand.

- Ask students to informally revisit the Kahoot! questions (science fiction elements) for this story, and give evidence in their table groups as to where the science fiction elements are in this particular story.

- Revisit the questions from the reading check. Instead of answering the next five in class, open up the *Padlet* once more, and categorize them under "literal" and "inferential." This is what your page should look like prior to students putting them in categories:

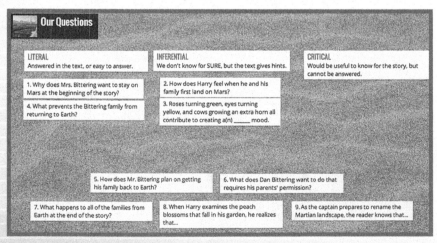

Discuss trends we notice:

- *Why were there no critical questions on this reading check?*

- *Why were there almost an equal number of literal and inferential questions?*

- *Why do teachers ask literal questions in their work for students?*

- *Why do teachers ask inferential questions? What do the answers show the teachers?*

- Circle our two (or three?) inferential questions, and let them know you'll be grading their individual answers to these, along with the literal questions we'd already answered in groups. (I gave them two separate marks — one for literal and one for inferential comprehension.)* See the resources for how students could turn in re-dos.

  Suggestion: If students get the literal questions wrong after your class discussion, simply have them answer other literal questions as a separate reading check. There is no need to "punish" them with grades for their behavior (in this case, not paying attention during group work) when the reading check is intended to see what they understand. It is valuable to see who does not have those literal questions correct, but a conversation needs to be had with the students if they are missing those types of questions. Ask students to answer a few new literal questions to see if they truly understand the text.

DAY THREE

Preparation:

- Each student will need available a copy of the story "Zero Hour" by Ray Bradbury. (A class set is fine.)

- Each student will need a place to write questions about the story.

- Each table group will need a device.

- Set up a page on *Padlet* or another site (*Linoit* or *Google* Doc) where students can add and see each other's responses, and you can edit and sort them.

Plans:

- Review *why* we are spending so much time asking questions. How will these questions help us in "real life," as well as in school?

- Begin reading the story — the students' job is to write questions as we read.

- After reading this one, students get into groups, share their myriad questions, and come up with one or two to which they want to know the answers.

- Each group receives a device on which to put their questions. This time, the definitions for each type of question should already be on the top of the *Padlet*. However, if students just put their questions any place, you can move them in the correct column together.

- Sort some of the questions, until you have at least *six* "inferential" questions listed.

- Have students whittle down the number to *four* "great inferential questions." I explained a "great" question as one we *think* we know the answer to, but we'd have to find hints from the author in the text itself.

The circled items on the image are the four questions we came up with.

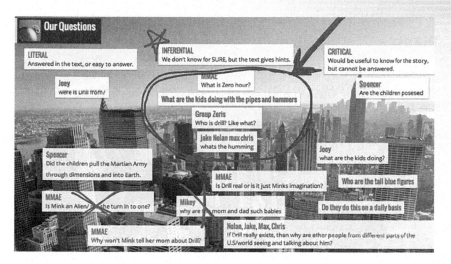

- Quickly delete the other questions (hint: click the trash can on each one, then go back and click "OK, Remove" on all of them for a quick clearing).

- Move each of the four remaining questions to a corner of the *Padlet*, signifying the corners where discussions will take place in the room.

- Ask students to bring their text to one corner of the room and be ready to answer that question using support from the text. (5-10 min)

- Have each group select a spokesperson to share the ideas of the group. (5-10 min)

DAY FOUR

Preparation:

- Each student will need available a copy of the story "Zero Hour" by Ray Bradbury. (A class set is fine.)

- Have a copy of the question listed below for each student.

- Set up four spaces in the room with labels — "Aliens," "Parents," "Children," and "Other."

Plans:

- Ask the following question of the students: "Who is responsible for the alien attack?"

- Give them the question below, and ask them to be ready to defend their answer.
  (This idea is from Michael W. Smith & Jeffrey D. Wilhelm's book *Fresh Takes on Teaching Literary Elements*, 2010.)
  Who was responsible for Earth being surprise attacked by aliens? You may choose any number percentages, as long as they all add up to 100%, or you may give 100% responsibility to one group.
  _____ the aliens _____ the children _____ the parents
  _____ someone else/other (Whom?_____)

- After students assign percentages, ask them to go to the four corners of the room, depending on whom they think is the MOST responsible, sharing textual evidence. (This can also be done as a fishbowl discussion.)

- Students write in response to this question after the discussion.

Our science fiction unit is a couple more days — feel free to add to what we've done and make it work for you! Of course, it's great to see the two movies, one older and one newer, that were made for "Zero Hour," and compare them, asking why the stories are different. At any point during these lessons, class fishbowl discussions would be valuable if you have the time, and students have shared questions suitable for a fishbowl discussion.

HANDOUTS/RESOURCES

Padlet

Kahoot Review

Sci Fi Book Trailers

"Evil Robot Monkey" Story

"Dark They Were and Golden-Eyed" Story

"Dark They Were" Reading Check

"Dark They Were" ReDo for Students

"Zero Hour" - Who is responsible?

WHAT MADE IT **MEMORABLE**

The questions that came from my students on these days, along with the evidence they provided for their answers, gave us an experience I won't soon forget. The best part of this journey is that they learned from each other. They learned that some of their questions are answered in the text if they look closely enough, some of their answers are debatable, depending on the evidence used, and some of their questions will never be answered, although they lead to more wondering, which is what we want.

Two small but important lessons learned included the fact that we don't always use question marks when we should, and we often use vague pronouns. Both of these can be obstacles to communicating with each other.

I absolutely loved it when one class moved one of their questions from "inferential" to "critical," as they realized something important: They were using their own background knowledge — instead of the text — to answer the question. They could not find any hints in the text as to the answer, so they decided they had to move it to the "critical" category. This is close reading and reflection at its best! Of course, students loved these days, as well. Their favorites were the two in which *they* created the questions. This has led us to ask students

113

to create their own questions from here on out. They suddenly are in more control of their own learning. I strive for the type of class in which my students learn from each other.

JOY KIRR *loves her family & friends, her profession, photography, geocaching, edcamps, reading, biking, music and life. She is in her 21st year of teaching and currently enjoys seventh grade English language arts in a suburb of Chicago. She was first a special education teacher working with deaf and hard-of-hearing students, and next became a reading specialist. She is a firm believer in student-driven learning.*

In the summer of 2014, she presented the keynote for the Passion-Driven Learning Strand at the K12 Online Conference. She hosted a "Master Class" on Genius Hour in Boston at the Building Learning Communities Education Conference and facilitated three more sessions on how to give more control over to students in 2015. Joy is a National Board Certified teacher.

Follow her on Twitter @JoyKirr.

Demystifying Poetry: 3-Step Poetry Analysis and "The Red Wheelbarrow"

Jori Krulder

"I want students to develop independence in analyzing poetry, moving beyond the misconception that a poem is a puzzle with one correct answer to the understanding that through thoughtful application of their perceptions and prior knowledge to various aspects of the text, they can create meaning competently on their own."

BECAUSE OF MY love for all things poetry, I was not prepared for student reaction to this subject when I first started teaching. I had visions of reading a beloved poem to the class and students joining me in impassioned discussion of the relevance and artistry embodied in each amazing stanza. We would explore ideas and, inspired by the amazing verse, we would write and read aloud our own poems. My actual experience could not have been further from this naïve dream.

I brought out one of my favorite poems: E. E. Cummings's "Anyone Lived in a Pretty How Town," read it aloud to the students and asked them: "What is this poem about?" When I was met with the profound silence and averted gaze of 33 sets of eleventh-grade eyes, I realized I had no idea what I was doing. Unfamiliar with the practice of wait time, I proceeded to fill the awkward silence with my interpretation of the poem, waxing rhapsodic about Cummings's social commentary and innovative use of grammar while they waited patiently for me to finish. When I stopped talking and asked them what they thought about the poem, they obligingly reiterated many of my points about the poem and I quickly realized this was not the way to teach analysis. I needed to figure out a way to put it into their hands.

I've since learned to anticipate that when the word "poetry" first comes up in my high school English classes, the groan that echoes through the room will not be one of delight. There are a brave few souls who profess undying love for poetry, but they are the exception rather than the rule. This turns out to be a reflection not just of our culture, but also of the type of exposure students have had to poetry.

Many teachers are not comfortable with teaching poetry analysis because of the way they've been taught – often with the presentation of a poem, followed by some frustrated silence, and a subsequent explanation by the teacher of what the "true" meaning of the poem is. Students are rarely given the opportunity to make meaning in poems for themselves – a process that takes time, practice, discussion, and much reassurance that they indeed have what it takes to interpret poetry themselves.

Over the years, through trial and error, I've developed many ways to open poetry up to my students, to make it more relevant and accessible, even the more difficult and less contemporary pieces. The 3-step poetry analysis is a method I use to introduce students to the process of looking into poetry. With both my "regular" English and AP Literature and Composition classes, I've found that once they've gotten their feet wet and started the conversation of what they notice in a poem, moving into deeper, more extensive analysis becomes possible. More importantly, they feel more comfortable taking on the challenge of making meaning for themselves.

Demystifying Poetry with 3-Step Poetry Analysis and "The Red Wheelbarrow"

LEARNING GOALS

BROAD **IMPLICATIONS**

Students will understand that:

- What they notice about a poem is important.

- Their perceptions and ideas are what create meaning in a poem.

- There are multiple "correct" interpretations of a poem's meaning.

KNOWLEDGE GAINED

Students will know:

- That annotation is more than just underlining or highlighting text – it involves writing their thoughts about the text.

- The definition of universal theme.

SKILLS ACQUIRED

Students will be able to:

- Read a poem independently and identify text that is meaningful to them.

- Discuss their thoughts and questions on various aspects of a poem.

- Use patterns of meaning in a poem to develop theme.

- Use evidence from a poem to support their interpretations.

JORI KRULDER

EVIDENCE OF LEARNING

- Student discussion throughout this process is one of the most essential performance tasks in assessing student understanding of and proficiency in poetry analysis. Various forms of discussion may be used: whole class, small group, pairs, fishbowl, or Socratic Seminar.

- Students will mark their observations on a whole class copy of the poem, explaining and discussing their thoughts about the text.

- Written evidence of students' progress in learning the analysis process will be in the notes they turn in at the end of class. These notes consist of:

    - A personal copy of the poem that should be annotated with observations on interesting or important things they notice about the text, and notes on each of the steps in the 3-Step process:

        - Initial impression of the poem.

        - A few words, lines, or phrases from the poem along with their ideas on them.

        - A theme for the poem, along with an explanation of what in the poem leads them to identifying this theme.

LEARNING PLAN

- Prior to this lesson, the class has done a few quick-writes and discussions on their experiences with poetry, including conceptions (and misconceptions) about the purposes of poetry and ways to read poetry. The most important idea for students to understand is that there is no one "right" interpretation for a poem – that rather, they create the meaning in a poem. This lesson begins their practice with this.

- First, I put the poem in front of students – on a SmartBoard, whiteboard, handout, etc. – and let them see and hear it.

STEP ONE: WHAT DO YOU NOTICE?

- The teacher explains that one of the keys to analyzing literature is reading it multiple times. When you're reading a book for the purposes of pure pleasure, you may only read it once through, just taking in the experience. This is the first step to reading poetry, as well.

- For the first step of reading a poem, read it once through, preferably aloud, and ask students: "What do you notice?" While students are reading and listening to the poem, their sole task is to jot down, on a separate sheet of paper, what they notice.

- Then we discuss. I usually have them set up a paper for notes, labeling each of the three steps. This process becomes less formal as they become more familiar with analyzing poetry, but for the sake of clarity and for assessment purposes, it's best to keep it delineated at first. Also, if students have had the time to formulate and write down their ideas before a discussion, it makes them more likely to participate fully.

- Although there are many discussion formats that I use – pair and share, group discussion, Socratic Seminar – I usually begin with a whole class discussion. This enables me to encourage and prompt student response. It's important to show students early on that no observation is too simple. With "The Red Wheelbarrow" students will often comment on the fact that it doesn't seem like a "real" poem,

JORI KRULDER

which leads to a teachable moment to consider and discuss what makes a poem a poem. We talk about the lack of rhyme, the weird line breaks, and just the general way the poem makes us feel, which for many of them is not much, at first. Acknowledge and validate all observations, even the ones offered in jest. It is important to keep the focus here on the students' perceptions – it may be tempting to comment further on something interesting a student has found, but restrain yourself and keep the conversation student-centered. Students need to see that they are the makers of meaning, and in this unfamiliar territory there are familiar landmarks: words and ideas.

- The discussion will begin to make students aware of the wide range of possible types of comments to make about poetry, and it is the perfect time to make a list of things you can say about a text, especially if you are using this lesson to begin teaching annotation. I usually have students write down the list as we discuss it, as this is one way of increasing attention to the information. The teacher elicits answers to the question, "What are some of the kinds of things we can say about poetry?" and then supplements them with any that are missing. The introductory list of possible comments includes: questions, connections, reactions/opinions, vocabulary issues, paraphrasing, and reflection. As students grow more proficient, I add ideas such as structure, rhythm, tone, and various literary devices. It is important to elicit ideas from students throughout this process rather than simply giving them a list so they develop their sense of proficiency with analysis. They need to know that they already have everything they really need to begin analyzing poetry.

STEP TWO: WHAT ELSE DO YOU NOTICE?

- The teacher then explains to the class that for step two of analyzing a poem, they will read through the poem again and mark in some way anything they notice that is important or interesting. They may underline or circle or draw an arrow pointing to the words of note. They may choose one word or a group of words – whatever jumps out at them. Next, they will go back and write a few words or symbols that show why they marked these words. They may write a question mark if they find a word or phrase that is confusing or they may make a comment about something that brings up an idea in their minds. Let them know they will be sharing these observations with the class.

- After giving students a few minutes to annotate the poem on their own, I usually model the annotation process on my document camera or SmartBoard, thinking aloud to the class as I circle words and phrases and write questions, connections, and observations on the poem. With "The Red Wheelbarrow," I wondered aloud why Williams chose the colors red and white, and what could possibly "depend" on a red wheelbarrow?

- Students should then take a few minutes to write down "Step Two" in their notes, copy down a few words or lines that they marked on the poem, and write a bit more in depth about their thoughts on the text. I tell them to write as much as they can, but not to worry about being formal – this step is intended to explore in writing their own ideas about particular parts of the text, just as I was doing out loud.

- Next, students come up to the board themselves and write comments on the poem. I usually hold off on the formal

JORI KRULDER

discussion until they've had a chance to turn the class copy of the poem into a wonderful mess of comments, partially because students need to see the range of ideas possible and partially because at first students feel more comfortable elucidating on their commentary from their seats. Eventually, though, many students will stand at the board, pointing at the poem, discussing such issues as the significance of the line breaks, the vivid picture the poem creates in their minds, and the briefness of the poem.

- The crucial part of this equation is that all thoughtful observations are valid and that we discuss, discuss, discuss. I ask questions to elicit further thinking about the details of the poem, such as: "That's interesting; why do you think he did that?" and "Explain what you mean by . . ." and "Tell me more about…." Occasionally, with classes that are less experienced with communication, I need to scaffold these skills more with techniques like fishbowl discussions, but, with patience and practice, students pick up on the discussion process, asking questions themselves and building on each others' ideas. It is in seeing the thought processes of others that students begin to see the possibilities for their own thoughts.

STEP 3: BRING IT ALL TOGETHER.

- After taking some time to discuss our diverse ideas, questions, and observations about the poem, patterns of meaning usually begin to emerge and I have students take a few minutes to write down what they think the overall meaning or theme of the poem is. The process of doing this by themselves is important, because it helps them gain confidence in their ability to independently create meaning in the poem.

- With "The Red Wheelbarrow," students have gone in interesting directions. One year, one of my AP Lit students was convinced that it was a treatise on communism, the wheelbarrow being a symbol for the underappreciated proletariat – and, after all, it *was* red.... Other students argued that the theme was more universal – a love note to all the simple things in life we tend to take for granted. No matter what level class I use this poem in, though, students begin to see the how the details they noticed in the various pieces of the poems can come together into a coherent idea that can apply to the world outside the poem. The relevance of the poem gradually becomes clear and they are the ones who created that clarity, by working together. Student-developed themes may start out as relatively simplistic and general, but you will be surprised at the depth they develop as students gain confidence in their analysis skills through this process.

JORI KRULDER

HANDOUTS/RESOURCES

Materials:

Poem, posted on the board for the whole class and handed out individually to students
"*The Red Wheelbarrow*" by William Carlos Williams
3-Step Poetry Analysis (posted on the board for students to copy and take notes from)

Step One: Read the poem once through, preferably aloud, and write down what you notice. Anything that seems important or interesting is fair game.

Step Two: Read the poem again a few more times and mark words, phrases, or lines that jump out at you as important or interesting. Next to the text you noted, write down a few words or phrases that explain why you marked that text.

Step Three: After discussing your and others' observations and ideas about the poem, consider any patterns of ideas you see and write down a theme for the poem. Write an explanation of this theme, using evidence from the poem to support your ideas.

WHAT MADE IT **MEMORABLE**

As a teacher of both Advanced Placement and "regular" English classes, I've learned that students come into my classroom with a wide range of ability and experience, and it's my job to meet them where they are and empower them to take their abilities to new levels.

Analysis is, at its heart, the practice of reading actively and thinking critically. Most of students' struggles with analysis stem from the fact that they get very little practice with reading a text actively and thinking about it independently. They are often accustomed to reading with the purpose of answering a specific set of questions and become very proficient at skimming the reading for those specific answers. While this skill is arguably useful, it does not even begin to address the need for being able look at a text — a poem, a newspaper article, a commercial advertisement — and come to some meaningful conclusions on one's own. And more importantly, skimming and answering questions drains away motivation, be it pleasure or just curiosity, to read and think about anything of one's own volition. Creating meaning for oneself becomes a rarer and rarer occurrence.

The 3-Step approach to poetry analysis has enabled me to give students a way into the conversation about meaning, and is an effective method of introducing close reading in any context, whether it's a primary document in American history, an article on genetic engineering, or an ad for a political campaign. Poetry is a surprisingly palatable medium to begin this process with, because its brevity, concentrated ideas, and layers of meaning lend themselves to the multiple readings and varied perspectives necessary for in-depth analysis. Also, the very lack of experience students have with analyzing poetry proves to be an advantage in this case, because, after taking the time to dispel the misconceptions students have about poetry, we can pretty much start the process from scratch. Step by step, students share their observations, learning the possibilities from listening to others and building on these ideas to create larger themes. Once students believe they have the power to make meaning themselves, we can begin the journey of making sense of the world.

JORI KRULDER *is heading into her 17*th *year of teaching English, having entered the field fueled by a passion for books and having continued because of her endlessly fascinating students. She taught English and reading for four years in urban San Diego before moving to Northern, CA to teach at a rural high school and to complete her MA in Education from Chico State University. In addition to reading and talking about literature, she's fueled by treasure hunting at yard sales, cycling, and some serious caffeine.*

Because communication is the key to making things better in education and our society as a whole, it is the core of Jori's pedagogy. Her students read a lot, write a lot, and discuss, discuss, discuss. They have scored well above the international average in all areas of the AP Literature and Composition exam. She has led workshops in discussion techniques that work across the curriculum and has published articles about teaching critical thinking skills through poetry on the Talks With Teachers *website AP Lit Help.*

Her ultimate goal is to build students' independence in their ability to understand and make themselves understood in this world.

Follow her on Twitter @JoriKrulder.

Those same students, with help, created digital narratives of their experiences that used images and music to communicate in an authentic way that has engaged every audience who has seen them.

This experience was an epiphany to me about using all students' inherent visual literacy as a bridge to textual literacy. Each student, regardless of cognitive or language ability, comes with a built-in literacy that he or she already uses to produce, consume and make meaning of the world.

This particular lesson, a paired reading of the Oscar-nominated short film "Madame Tutli-Putli" with T. Coraghessan Boyle's flash fiction story "The Hit Man," has evolved over five years. My students co-created it with me, as we identified the most interesting texts and questions.

I've always been a T. C. Boyle fan and I love film, so they seemed to go together for me. "The Hit Man" is particularly appealing to high school students because it takes the idea of the assassin — an idea so popular that the video game series *Assassin's Creed* is built around it — and uses it to define Death as a mercenary sociopath. The film is interesting because it examines the disappearance of everyone on a train, much like the "Left Behind" or other Rapture-type genres, but without any religious overtones. (Be aware of one crude gesture a third of the way in, which makes this most suitable for juniors and seniors.)

Building Bridges with Visual Literacy
LEARNING GOALS

BROAD **IMPLICATIONS**

Students will understand that:

- Reading is strategic and purposeful, that we read to see ourselves and

    - To understand human behavior.

    - To vicariously experience life in ways we never have to in real life.

    - To learn empathy for others.

    - As C.S. Lewis said, "To know that we are not alone."

KNOWLEDGE GAINED

Students will know that:

- Readers can transfer the same set of skills they use to decode film and video to decode complex or difficult texts.

SKILLS ACQUIRED

Students will be able to:

- Notice the cognitive moves they are making to understand film.

- Explicitly name those moves that make meaning and create understanding.

- Create a heuristic showing the relationship between visual and print literacy (e.g., for both, it's important to re-read to make meaning).

SHANNA PEEPLES

EVIDENCE OF LEARNING

- Students will create leveled questions for the film and the text.

  - **Level one** questions are text-based and answers can be found within the text.

  - **Level two** questions are inferential and require the reader to create their own meaning using what they know in conjuction with what the text reveals.

  - **Level three** questions are universal questions that are inspired by a text, but the text doesn't determine the question.

- Students will create digital and written narratives of either an event from their own lives or a fictional story of their own creation

- Students will co-create a rubric, with teacher's feedback, to evaluate the quality of the finished writing. You can use an existing rubric as a model for them, but I've found that it's most engaging when students co-create a rubric of three to four criteria and assign point values.

- Students will create an original piece of writing based upon their own self-generated questions inspired by these texts.

An extension for advanced learners is to have students create their own film and story using the ideas sparked by their reading. Students will co-create a rubric, with teacher's feedback, to judge the narrative's quality.

- If possible, students will view models of finished work to guide their thinking and planning.

- This can be extended further by using feature films and literature. For example, using video clips from *Apocalypse Now* with the novel *The Heart of Darkness*.

LEARNING PLAN

- Ideally, this lesson is spread over three 50-minute class periods.

- In order to preview and prepare students for the film, "Madame Tutli-Putli," focus on the following:

Things To Notice

- The various objects and bags that Madame Tutli-Putli has with her; she's bent over with the weight of them and is bringing a lot of "stuff."

- The chess game — it changes every time there's a bump, yet the players adjust (metaphor alert!).

- The characters each have objects — they are clues to the type of people they are.

- The sun literally sets and the screens fades to black for several seconds.

- After the mysterious green gas/smoke, there seems to be a moose that is hit by a train and then Madame Tutli-Putli comes to. We see that all the other passengers are gone, as is all of her baggage. There is nothing left. Then she seems to have a memory of the other passengers being operated on. Then a skeletal face that makes a "shhhh" motion at her.

- Everything is dark until she gets to the club car where she sees the moth again.

SHANNA PEEPLES

- The moth transitions with the frame into a whiteout.

- We see what looks like her figure transposed over the wings of a moth.

- There is a lengthy fade to black.

- We see what may be a sunrise beginning to come up over the trees.

- Students use the first day to watch the film and take notes. It's best to watch the film at least twice, if possible, just watching it to see what happens the first time. Students should begin noting things about it on the second and third viewings and capturing their ideas on their note-taking foldables.

- Preview and prepare the students for the the short story "The Hit Man."

Things to Notice:

- Subheadings.

- Diction changes: "wastes," for example, contrasted with "filial" and "loathes and abominates."

- Short sentences.

- Character description.

- Fragmented narrative.

- Students read the short story, taking notes on what they notice as they read.

- Students create leveled questions for the film and the text.

This is easiest to teach by using the story of Cinderella. Students recall the story with a partner or group. The teacher then leads them into making sample leveled questions as a guide like these:

- **Level one:** Who is in Cinderella's family?

- **Level two:** Why doesn't Cinderella's father intervene for her?

- **Level three:** Is there such a thing as love at first sight?

- Have struggling students create a simple foldable that helps them to separate levels. Just fold a standard piece of paper into thirds and label each with a level.

- Students use this to take notes on the film and text. They can turn the paper over and label the other three columns:

  - What repeats?

  - What is the tone (or "feeling," for struggling students) and how do I know?

  - Who gets the most attention and what stands out about them?

- After students have practiced thinking critically about both texts, they are ready to discuss the relationship of film to text. The teacher creates an anchor chart from the discussion that explicitly shows the relationship. A simple T-chart is easiest for this: write "What did I do to understand the film?" on one side of the T-chart and "What did I do to understand the text?" on the other side.

- Next, students create their own questions in partners or groups. The teacher should give an example of each type of question. After partners have created several questions for each text, they identify a level two or three question that

SHANNA PEEPLES

they are both drawn to for use as a personalized writing prompt.

- Students then take this question through the writing process individually, and can later share their writing with their groups or partners.

HANDOUTS/RESOURCES

ESSENTIAL QUESTIONS

For struggling students and language learners:

How is watching film and video like reading?

What can I learn from stories that will help me with my life?

All students:

How can I use a skill I'm already good at (reading images and video) to increase my reading skills?

How can learning to read film help me learn to read text?

What are the specific skills of analysis and how can they help me in other parts of my life?

How can I use what I know about how real people behave to understand why characters in film and stories behave the way they do?

How do you find a story's theme? Why does it matter?

Advanced students:

How does a director work like an author?

How does film inform text?

How does structure affect meaning?

How do film and literature hold a mirror up to life?

Discussion Questions — Film

1. What is the significance of the priest and the hit man wearing black?

2. Why do you think only three of the characters have names?

3. What is the significance of money in this story?

Recurring Images/Ideas

- the colors black and gold

- the hitman's hood

- the cyclical nature of life and death as well as its random nature

- incongruity in the hitman's life: he is an assassin as well as a seemingly suburban husband and father

- the story's episodic structure

Viewing Notes

- An obscene gesture is made at 4:40-4:50; there is a somewhat disturbing image of an organ being removed at 11:30-35.

- Each of these texts tries to explain the fundamental mystery of death. Boyle's story personifies it as an assassin who was an abused child. The film sees it as a toxin released by unknown forces or persons. The sense of death's unpredictability ties both texts together.

Discussion Questions — Story

1. What does Madame Tutli-Putli's baggage reveal about her character?

2. What is the significance of the chess game? What happens?

3. What do you notice about each of the other passengers on the train? What kinds of objects do they have around them and what do these objects suggest about them?

SHANNA PEEPLES

4. How does the director communicate Madame Tutli-Putli's fear when...?

5. How does the film create suspense for the audience and show...?

6. Even though the video has no words, the director is able to generate emotion through the actions of the characters. Which actions are the most important in understanding the personalities of each character? Who would you want to sit by on the train? Who would you avoid? Why?

7. What clues does the director give us at the end of the video about what happened to Madame Tutli-Putli?

Recurring Images

- chess piece
- light/lamps
- moth
- windows
- darkness/ shadows
- mud
- colors — blue/red/green

WHAT MADE IT **MEMORABLE**

Providing students with small, consistent successes motivates them. Nobody wants to feel like a failure — that hurts. It's also hard, if you are a student who struggles with reading comprehension, to continually force yourself to work with words.

This lesson shows students that they already possess a tool to unlock challenging texts. Leveraging their visual literacy as well as the inferential skills they already possess allows them to feel a sense of control over their own learning. They come to feel confident in themselves as learners who can make meaning, draw inferences, and apply these skills across texts. That, in my experience, is really powerful for students who feel shut out of learning. You can see it on their faces as they begin to use simple, repeatable strategies to understand the film. They don't realize, until you make it explicit to them, that they already view film strategically because they've taken it for granted.

Making the strategies, like re-reading for example, explicit helps them to name and then repeat those strategies. All of these practices seem so simple, but deploying them strategically and then having students use them deliberately gives students access to texts of all kinds.

For many students, reading is a pseudo-concept. They know they are supposed to "get" the text, but they don't know how or why they should even try, So they behave pseudo-conceptually by forcing themselves to come up with wild inferences that aren't based in either reality or in the text. They see accomplished readers — or their teachers — seemingly performing a magic trick with text by extracting deep meaning with little to no effort. As a way of imitating what they've always seen — and what, to some extent, has always made them feel ashamed — they attempt to make meaning by connecting the text to whatever idea immediately occurs to them. Then they will pull text that doesn't support the inference because they've been drilled on finding "textual evidence" for test prep since the third grade. And this is the good news for the ones who try. Others simply shut down, too overwhelmed by frustration and repeated failure to hazard an attempt.

And by the way, this is not only a "struggling reader" or "ELL" problem — it's an AP problem too. In some ways, AP students are the worst because they're such accomplished players at the game of school. They know how to slyly and subtly con their teachers into answering their own questions, which they then regurgitate back in writing. When asked to make their own meaning, they blank because

Harper's Magazine article "What Is Literature? In Defense of the Canon" at http://bit.ly/1e2oHa9).

The author of the article about Tartt's work poses the same question I ask my students to ponder each year: "What makes a work of literature, and who gets to decide?"

Since mine is a workshop classroom where our primary focus is writing, students choose the books they read. That is not to say we do not read high-quality complex literature or read literature as a whole class. We read many passages together and learn skills that students then apply to their independent reading and the novels they discuss in book clubs four times a year.

My goal with books is to develop readers, and too many of my students did not read when I made all the decisions about their reading. However, many of my students do not know how to choose books they might enjoy or books with enough complexity to challenge their thinking. The drive to fulfill my goal to develop readers becomes multifaceted. Allowing choice means I must constantly be on the lookout for richly written passages that we can study, and I must read volumes of high-quality literature, YA and adult alike, so that I may match my adolescent readers with good books.

I love the last paragraph of *The Goldfinch* because I can use it for several learning opportunities. This short passage can teach us much about what makes a work of literature. I agree with researcher and reading theorist Louise Rosenblatt: "Students need to be helped to have personally satisfying and personally meaningful transactions with literature. Then they will develop the habit of turning to literature for the pleasures and insights it offers."

And that's the whole point, isn't it? We help our students love literature so they learn from it as we do.

What Makes a Work of Literature?
LEARNING GOALS

BROAD IMPLICATIONS

Students will understand that:

- Literature by definition moves us, connects us as human-kind, and inspires us to think.

- Good writing requires structure and form.

- Good sentences are the foundation of good writing.

KNOWLEDGE GAINED

Students will know:

- Terms: literary criticism, reader's response, syntax, effect.

- Literature has a standard of excellence.

- Sentence structure is the basis of good writing.

SKILLS ACQUIRED

Students will be able to:

- Read and discuss literary criticism and a passage of literature.

- Respond to a passage of literature and discuss their response with peers.

- See variety in sentence structures and discuss how those structures affect meaning.

- Practice a variety of sentence structures in their own writing.

- Begin to determine the quality in the books they choose to read.

AMY RASMUSSEN

EVIDENCE OF LEARNING

- Students will take on the role of literary critic as they find a passage in their independent reading that they justify as literature.

- Performance Task: Students will provide an annotated copy of the passage, which shows their understanding of the variety of sentence structures, and they will write a one page critique in which they assert whether the book may be defined as literature, or not, using a variety of sentence structures in their own writing.

Other Evidence:

- Participation in class discussions.

- Notebook writing.

LEARNING PLAN

Preparation

A day or two before the lesson, give students a copy or link to both pieces of literary criticism, "What Is Literature? In Defense of the Canon" and "It's Tartt, But Is It Art?" Ask students to read and annotate in preparation for a Socratic Seminar or Harkness Discussion about these texts. The guiding question is: What makes a work of literature?

DAY 1

- Tell students the title and the goal of the lesson and post the essential questions.

- Facilitate a Socratic Seminar or Harkness Discussion around the two texts students have read as homework.

- Discussion Debrief. Toward the end of the class period, ask students to write a reflection in their writer's notebooks.

"How has the discussion helped your understanding of what makes a work of literature?" "What do you understand now that you did not before?"

DAY 2

- Remind students of the title and the goal of the lesson and revisit the essential questions.

- Use any, or all, of the quotations about literature (See **Handout 1**) to continue the discussion about what makes a work of literature.

  - Option 1: Post a quotation on the board and ask students to defend, challenge or qualify it in their writer's notebooks. Write for five minutes. Turn and talk with a neighbor about their responses.

  - Option 2: Print the handout. Give a copy to each small group and ask students to read the quotations and then discuss, agreeing or disagreeing with the assertions. 10-15 minutes.

- Tell students that they will now read a passage from *The Goldfinch*. (**Handout 2**) First, they should read and determine a specific sentence or phrase that speaks to them. Explain that if literature is designed to teach us about life, humanity, etc. (as discussed the day before) then we should pay particular attention to how it does that and be prepared to write in response to literature. Ask students to respond to the text, either in its entirety or to the sentence or phrase that they think is powerful or poignant. Write for 8-10 minutes. The teacher may choose to have students share with a neighbor or ask for volunteers to share their responses.

AMY RASMUSSEN

- Next, ask students to read the passage again. This time they should pay particular attention to the author's craft and how she uses devices and varies the syntax. Give students several minutes to read and annotate the passage. Ask students to turn and talk with their neighbor about their reading and annotations. As a class, share and discuss student observations. Allow this to lead into a discussion on how the author varies the syntax and crafts meaning.

- Then, have students unpack the text:

    - Consider having students make a list of the sentences, so they can see the variety in sentence length.

    - Ask: *"What else do you notice?"* (Possible responses: use of dashes, parentheses, semicolons, colons, beginning a sentence with *but* and *and*, repetition of *that*.) Ask: "Why? What is the effect?"

    - Tell students the Performance Task for this lesson, answer any questions, and assign a due date.

HANDOUTS/RESOURCES

Prior to the lesson, the teacher should read both pieces of literary criticism to better his/her understanding of the whole of the texts included in this lesson. Give students a copy of these texts, or links to them, so that they may read and annotate in preparation for Day 1 of this lesson.

- Arthur Krystal. *"What Is Literature? In Defense of the Canon,"* published in *Harper's Magazine*, March 2014. http://bit.ly/1e2oHa9.

- Evgenia Peretz. "It's Tartt, But Is It Art?" published in *Vanity Fair*, July 2014. http://vnty.fr/1oN2Fd3.

Students need writer's notebooks or clean paper for writing in response to questions and reading.

Handout 1

To subvert is not the aim of literature, its value lies in discovering and revealing what is rarely known, little known, thought to be known, but in fact, not very well known of the truth of the human world. It would seem that truth is the unassailable and most basic quality of literature.

GAO XINGJIAN, NOBEL LECTURE, 2000

What matters in the end in literature, what is always there, is the truly good. And — though played out forms can throw up miraculous sports...what is good is always what is new, in both form and content. What is good forgets whatever models it might have had, and is unexpected; we have to catch it on the wing.

V. S. NAIPAUL, READING & WRITING

The things that are said in literature are always the same. What is important is the way they are said.

JORGE LUIS BORGES, THE PARIS REVIEW, WINTER-SPRING 1967

[Literature is] a process of producing grand, beautiful, well-ordered lies that tell more truth than any assemblage of facts.

JULIAN BARNES, THE PARIS REVIEW, WINTER 2000

If the purpose of literature is to illuminate human nature, the purpose of fantastic literature is to do that from a wider perspective. You can say different things about what it means to be human if you can contrast that to what it means to be a robot, or an alien, or an elf.

JO WALTON, INTERVIEW, LITERATURA FANTASTICO, NOV. 22, 2012

I would be wonderful with a 100-year moratorium on literature talk, if you shut down all literature departments, close the book reviews, ban the critics. The readers should be alone with the books, and if anyone dared to say anything about them, they would be shot or imprisoned

AMY RASMUSSEN

right on the spot. Yes, shot. A 100-year moratorium on insufferable literary talk. You should let people fight with the books on their own and rediscover what they are and what they are not. Anything other than this talk.

PHILIP ROTH, *The Guardian*, Dec. 13, 2005

A piece of literature can be many things but first of all it must capture its audience. You need to seduce people, entice them into a world of beauty and horror, light and shadow, of passion, of romance, of mystery. That's the magic of it. Beyond that, of course, you can open a dialogue about the ideas which interest you, but first of all you absolutely must get inside people's minds. CARLOS RUIZ ZAFON, "Carlos Ruiz Zafon's love letter to literature", New Zealand Listener, Mar. 14, 2013

Handout 2

PASSAGE FROM *THE GOLDFINCH*

Whatever teaches us to talk to ourselves is important: whatever teaches us to sing ourselves out of despair. But the painting has also taught me that we can speak to each other across time. And I feel I have something very serious and urgent to say to you, my non-existent reader, and I feel I should say it as urgently as if I were standing in the room with you. That life — whatever else it is — is short. That fate is cruel by maybe not random. That Nature (meaning Death) always wins but that doesn't mean we have to bow and grovel to it. That maybe even if we're not always so glad to be here, it's our task to immerse ourselves anyway: wade straight through it, right through the cesspool, while keeping eyes and hearts open. And in the midst of our dying, as we rise from the organic and sink back ignominiously into the organic, it is a glory and a privilege to love what Death doesn't touch. For if disaster and oblivion have followed this painting down through time — so too has love. Insofar as it is immortal (and it is) I have a small, bright, immutable part in that immortality. It exists; and it keeps on existing. And I add my own love to the history of people who have loved beautiful things, and looked out for them, and pulled them from the fire, and sought them when they were lost, and tried to preserve them and save them while passing them along literally from hand to hand, singing out brilliantly from the wreck of time to the next generation of lovers, and the next (771).

Tartt, Donna. The Goldfinch. Little, Brown, 2015. Print.

WHAT MADE IT **MEMORABLE**

The first time I introduced students to *The Goldfinch* passage I had them annotate, labeling the literary and rhetorical devices and the grammatical structures we learned in class. There are many: anaphora, appositive phrase, personification, parenthetical aside, metaphor, polysyndeton, and parallel structure. I know now that students learn much more about how language works by moving beyond labels. They need to know how the words and sentences work to make meaning much more than what we call the devices. They need to know that we find ourselves in literature, and sometimes as writers we find our voices.

In their responses to that last paragraph from *The Goldfinch*, a few of my students wrote the following:

"For if disaster and oblivion have followed this painting down through time — so too has love."

The sentence reminds me of the circle of hate in our community, state, nation, and sometimes our homes every single day. It's because of love that we may also hate. If you love someone and something happens to that person, the only thing you can feel is anger, anguish, hate. If your son goes to war and then dies by the enemy's hand, you may want, even get, revenge. What about the enemy's family? At that moment, the circle of hate will start anew. The painting is a metaphor for something more. Something to do with generations, ages, emotions, time. Maybe there's a connection with today's world of murders, deaths, thievery, and wars. ~Marques

"That maybe even if we're not always so glad to be here, it's our task to immerse ourselves anyway; wade straight through it, right through the cesspool, while keeping eyes and hearts open."

AMY RASMUSSEN

"We do not appreciate our planet earth, our life on it. This earth is the only planet that has life and beautiful nature. We do not appreciate it. Generations and generations, and each generation changes the earth and changes its priorities. My generation is all about technology. In social media I have seen teens post pictures about not wanting to be here, not wanting to live here. Here where the sun's rays heat our skin and make us sweat or chill us in the darkness. The world is not perfect, and it never will be. We have to see the positive. There are people around the world longing for their loved ones. Look! You have yours. See the positive." ~Sandra

"That fate is cruel but not random."

"Since I was a little girl, I have heard the phrase 'everything happens for a reason.' When I read this sentence, something my father taught me very well finally made sense. I had always wondered why I never got the chance to meet my grandpa, my dad's dad. Then, my dad sat me down and told me that when he was 17, his dad was shot in the head and died instantly. You can imagine, it was hard on the whole family emotionally and economically. My father at a very young age came to the U.S., so he could provide for his family, and while growing up was hard on him, my dad said that because of his father's death he became hardworking, honest, mature. My dad said maybe I wouldn't even be here if it weren't for my grandfather's death. Maybe fate is as cruel as we think, but it also draws a path that is already made for us." ~Catherine

"That Nature (meaning Death) always wins, but that doesn't mean we have to grovel to it."

"Death is inevitable, and I am a great manipulator. I make myself believe I am not scared of death. That I am not the kind of person who lives day by day as if it were my last. In reality, I would rather go home, watch a mind-blowing episode of Prison Break, and go to bed. I live with a mindset that chains me down, restrains me, keeps me isolated in my cubicle of a room, from enjoying life. Because 'Nature always wins,' I must remove this insipid fear of mine and dump it on the moon, the farther the

better, and make myself believe that living life will be the death of me. And that is okay. From now on, I will take over the rein." ~Jessica

I love to read this kind of thinking. If you'll notice, most of these students also included an interesting variety of sentences just in these quickwrite-type reflections. I know the more I help them discover important literary skills student writing improves right along with their thinking about the text itself.

The Goldfinch spans decades in a thick 771 pages. I did not expect any of my students to read the whole of the novel. Then one day my copy disappeared. It was gone from its nest, right under the potted plant on the bookshelf in the front of my room. Doreen had swiped it, and by the time I knew she had it, she had read about half way through. When I conferred with her about her reading, Doreen rated Donna Tartt's work a 9 out of 10, saying she found the story compelling although it dragged in places. (Spoken like an up-and-coming literary critic.) She said she finally felt like she could recognize skill when it came to writing. "I'll be more careful in my own writing now," Doreen told me.

Good enough for me.

AMY RASMUSSEN

AMY RASMUSSEN *teaches AP English Language and Composition at Lewisville High School in Lewisville, TX. She has a BA in Literature and an ME in Education from the University of North Texas. She is a member of NCTE and serves on the board of NTCTELA, her local affiliate. The energetic lives of her seven young adult children and the antics of her little grandchildren contend with reading as Amy's favorite pastime. She is a National Writing Project teaching consultant and writes at the blog www.ThreeTeachersTalk.com.*

Follow her on Twitter @AmyRass.

Literary 3x3: Literary Analysis Remixed & Reshuffled

Dan Ryder

"They should find themselves equipped with a powerful analytical tool and dynamic synthesis process that will evolve throughout the school year. They will be able to distill a text down to its most essential concepts and themes, identify the benefits and challenges of collaborative analysis, and recognize trends across a collection of analyses."

WE NEEDED TO *move.*

I've experienced exceptional intellects in my classes over the years: powerful problem solvers, efficient students, dynamic thinkers. Yet a new challenge awaited me: the largest student enrollment, the greatest number of sections, and the highest concentration of artists ever assembled in the history of AP English Literature and Composition at Mt. Blue. (Granted, this is only about a twenty-five year history, but milestones are milestones and should be heralded with great pomp and circumstance.)

Painters and cartoonists, dancers and directors, improvisers and animators, composers and crafters, sculptors and designers filled three sections of my typically one section course. I was accustomed to working with creatives — after all, it is a literature course — but with such an intense concentration of artistic spirits and capacity for seeing the world through unfamiliar lenses, the typical seminar wasn't going to cut it.

We needed to move. We needed to make.

For some reason, I forewent the Internet in my search for inspiration and delved into that shelf most colleagues seem to have: the dusty professional development materials one always intends to use but forgets because *Google*. Trapped between a binder of peer coaching routines and a thin volume on early 2000s digital citizenship, nestled in the pages of a College Board AP Lit instructional guide, I found reference to William Melvin Kelley's Literary 3x3 strategy.

A brief paragraph captured the essential features of the Literary 3x3 summarization technique: Three three-word sentences. Avoid prepositions and articles. Make every word count. There were other parameters and further investigation revealed still more constraints, but those mattered little because the catalyst was right there. Upon finishing Shelley's *Frankenstein*, students would craft Literary 3x3s, transfer the words to Post-It notes, and then remix them into new configurations to see what new notions emerged. The Literary 3x3s would dovetail with our work with diction, the importance of connotation and the weight of words, and an ongoing emphasis on intention.

We needed to move. We needed to make. We needed to collaborate.

Sitting in front of a prototype, a pile of stickies in hand, it became clear that while I had a tactile and visual experience shaping up, it was still a solitary experience. Students would be sharing their work with one another — yet I could see it falling short of engaging students in the way I was imagining. I built another sample L3x3, happening to use another color of Post-Its, and the solution revealed itself: mix the L3x3s. Doing so would uncover new perspectives, expose trends, require more authentic collaboration, and elevate the mash-up remix culture in the room.

The Post-Its proved a problem. They were small, started curling after several movements, and were difficult to keep track of if the lesson took longer than a day. Cue the index cards. We would be able to number them on the back, keeping track of the original creation and treating each like a puzzle to solve when passed.

And, if I'm being honest, I was also seeing the dollar signs attached to all of those sticky notes and this felt too important to limit to my wallet's boundaries.

We needed to move. We need to make. We needed to collaborate. We needed to sustain.

The first L3x3 lesson on *Frankenstein* proved a success and the students requested another round the following class. Thus, we engaged Byron and Percy Bysshe Shelley through L3x3s as well, distilling "Prometheus" and "Prometheus Unbound," respectively, with "Ozymandias" added for good measure.

This is when the index cards proved their value and the L3x3s truly demonstrated their power. We could build decks and keep them over time. We could continue to grow them, adding in more ideas, finding more connections. We could treat them like collectible card games, with battles and challenges galore. And they could be easily stored in ziplock bags in a filing cabinet drawer.

Students were not only able to remix a single work, but to combine sets of L3x3s to identify core themes and concepts, in this case to show similarities between these Romantics. Relationships between the works became more tangible and, in a way, malleable. With a slide and a flip, a word shifted here, a phrase there, students were able to change the tone, the intentions of the original, evaluate effectiveness and degrees of congruency. And laugh. A great many terrible ideas and constructions could be formed, giggled and guffawed over, then shuffled away.

Moments later, sublime serendipity would strike as three, four, or five L3x3s, unified to unlock insights heretofore hidden, their creators basking in the epiphany, an act of making yielding understanding.

3x3: Literary Analysis Remixed & Reshuffled
LEARNING GOALS

BROAD **IMPLICATIONS**

Students will understand that:

- Identifying the most essential themes and concepts of a text can reveal hidden truths behind an author's intentions.

- Simplicity and clarity may be just as challenging to craft as complexity and enigma.

- Evaluation and creation may serve a valuable role in the process of analysis.

- Summary of a text is not limited to the narrative events of a text.

- Collaboration presents both challenges and opportunities in analytical and creative endeavors.

- Identifying trends across a collection of works can provide validity.

- Remixing an idea is not an act of theft but an act of collaboration.

KNOWLEDGE GAINED

Students will know:

- That an effective summary captures the spirit of a text.

- That powerful, active language proves more useful than dry, passive language.

- That connotative meanings add depth and intention to a text beyond denotative meetings.

SKILLS ACQUIRED

Students will be able to:

- Identify central themes or ideas of a text.

- Express central ideas of a text using only nine words.

- Assess and evaluate effectiveness of diction and structure.

- Collaborate with others to resolve a common challenge.

EVIDENCE OF LEARNING

- Students will solve summary puzzles of well-known texts to orient to Literary 3x3 thinking.

- Students will individually generate a summary in three three-word sentences that captures the essential themes and ideas of the text, a.k.a. L3x3s.

- Upon sharing these Literary 3x3s, students will transfer the words to index cards, thus creating an initial L3x3 "deck."

- Students will experiment with their decks to discover other arrangements of their words that reveal both congruent and incongruent summaries of the text.

- Students will swap decks with other students, "solve" the decks and check for effectiveness, providing feedback.

- Students will identify and map trends across the L3x3s on display.

- Students will mix decks in pairs, triads, or other configurations to explore possibilities and reveal other insights of the text through remixes and new creations.

DAN RYDER

- Students will document their L3x3s and reflect on the experience by addressing one or more essential questions via writing, video, or either an analog or digital audio medium.

- Optional extension: students may create original works inspired by the L3x3s content.

LEARNING PLAN

- Prior to lesson's inception, students should have had experience reading the text to be analyzed. However, once students are familiar with the tools and processes, this lesson proves highly effective with cold readings as well.

- Open the lesson with exemplar L3x3s decks of well-known films and texts such as *Harry Potter*, *Star Wars*, *Spider-Man* and *Twilight*. Place them on various student desks and ask them to solve the puzzle, explaining that they need to create three three-word sentences from the nine words on the individual index cards. It will be helpful to display an example for all to see, i.e.:

  - Tornado transports girl.

  - Adventures reveal strengths.

  - Discovers home persists.

- During discussion of L3x3s, be certain to point out these are effective L3x3s but there are no "correct" answers. Many, many possible solutions exist.

- Review criteria for an effective L3x3:

  - Three three-word "sentences": loose grammar.

  - Powerful, meaningful diction: consider connotation vs denotation.

- Every word counts: avoid prepositions and articles.

- Guided by annotations, sketchnotes, and doodles as well as source text in question, students generate L3x3s in whatever medium desired.

- Review the L3x3s as they are generated. After the teacher gives their work the thumbs up, students may then transfer that L3x3 to nine index cards, one word per card.

- Upon forming the deck, students should lay out their L3x3s and then number the cards on the back side 1-9, so as to create an answer key. Students should also put their initials in the lower right corner of the numbered side of the deck. On the word side of the cards, students should put the full or abbreviated title, name of the text in the lower left hand corner, and the author or creator's name in the lower right. This is vital for later as L3x3s decks multiply.

- Challenge students to remix their L3x3s into other arrangements to discover new insights.

- Ask students to swap decks and try to "solve" partners' L3x3s. Have students provide meaningful feedback to partners.

- After initial decks have been created and swapped, ask students to lay out all L3x3s as they were originally intended. Students then circulate the room looking for trends and outliers.

- While looking for trends and outliers, put each observation on a separate sticky note. Work as a class to map and organize these observations. Hint: using different colors for trends and outliers (either in ink or on sticky note) can help with visual thinking.

DAN RYDER

- After noting the trends, have students form pairs and combine their decks. Ask them to create a L3x3 from the mixed deck. If they are unable to do so, ask the group to combine with another group until they are able to create a series of L3x3 remixes. Each success should be documented through notes or images.

- Students then use the decks to explore any number of L3x3 games and battles. Emphasize documentation of understandings and experiences via digital image, written record, video or audio recording.

  - War. Mix decks and split in two. Each player lays out a card. Discuss which word is more central to the text. If players cannot agree, lay out the next cards and continue the discussion. The winner of each round collects the cards.

  - Fastest Fingers. Mix decks and split them evenly amongst players. The first player to lay out any three or more words that makes a cogent summary and can justify it wins.

  - L6x6 & L2x2. Try new reconfigurations and constraints to see what they unlock.

- After these explorations, students reflect individually via written, audio or video media, answering any one or more of the essential questions for the lesson.

- Optional Extension: Challenge students to use L3x3 remixes as starting points for original works inspired by a source text and exploring like themes and ideas. Challenge them to create a work that seems the original creator, while still being traceable to the L3x3, could create it.

WHAT MADE IT **MEMORABLE**

Adopting the Literary 3x3 remix strategy into my regular repertoire proved quite a pivot point in my classroom. Visual, kinesthetic formats for discussion and analysis have become the norm rather than a change of pace. Similarly, creativity and making are now central to my formative assessment design, not merely signals of a summative project. It's hard to say if the L3x3 revolution caused that shift or if I arrived at L3x3s because change was already underway. Regardless of the root, the effects have been widespread.

Students now regularly post L3x3s on their blogs, using other students' L3x3s as sources for commentary and springboards for new explorations. Critical dialogue opens up around which words best suit the L3x3, with impassioned cases made all around. Grand experiments in crafting original works inspired by source texts incorporate the language of the L3x3s, resulting in student-generated pieces that seem, at a glance, fresh from the unpublished archives of Joyce and Eliot, Woolf and Shelley. Remixes and mashups of video and audio sources tend to first start with students identifying nine key moments, the idea of chunking the thoughts into three moment phrases transferring over.

While I often assign them as evidence of understanding, just as many L3x3s seem to be generated these days without my say-so. Many students remark that L3x3s have become a habit of analytical mind, a necessary step in the process of understanding a text. Ninth grade Humanities students use them to tackle non-fiction prior to discussions, while AP Lit students write them in the margins of their test booklets. L3x3s work their way into writing workshops and the design process, becoming highly effective tools for feedback, students crafting L3x3s of peer drafts, the peers then remixing or reimagining those L3x3s to inform the next iteration. A missing card from a deck twelve, fifteen texts high becomes cause for panic, while building nimble, dynamic decks becomes a bragging right.

DAN RYDER

Nine words. Nine index cards. One Sharpie. It seems somewhat ridiculous such simple tools can yield such powerful results, but I suppose the Literary 3x3 only further testifies to the power of intention, the strength in collaboration, and the art of the remix.

———

DAN RYDER, is a *high school English teacher by title, idea-wrangler, design-thinker, school change-maker and student-empowerer by practice. He has spent the better part of twenty years teaching English at Mt. Blue Campus in rural college town, Farmington, Maine. In that time he has piloted a student-led personalized learning program, shepherded graphic novels and a pop culture elective into the curriculum, and co-created a ninth grade interdisciplinary Humanities course. His classroom practice continues to evolve, bringing an empathy-fueled, human-centered design thinking approach to teaching and learning, blending digital and analog tools and experiences in an effort to foster critical thinkers and problem solvers.*

Particularly proud of his ability to make things up as he goes, Dan also directs the high school improv comedy troupe, Mt. Blue Curtain Raisers and blogs, tweets, and social medias as co-founder of Maine-based Wicked Decent Learning. He has delivered workshops and keynotes around the country on design thinking, improvisation, educational technology and progressive education, including sessions at Maine's ACTEM ed tech conference, SXSWedu, Stanford's d.School, The Ellis School for Girls Active Learning Summit, and Mount Vernon Institute for Innovation's FUSE experience.

Follow him on Twitter @WickedDecent.

April Awesomeness Poetry Challenge

Joshua Stock

"I want them to determine the effectiveness of a poem in relation to other poems and support their position with evidence from the text. They will use the views of their classmates to strengthen their position and actively participate in moving the dialogue forward."

MIDDLE SCHOOL STUDENTS are a tad emotional — much like a nuclear bomb is a tad destructive or a baby panda is a tad adorable. They experience a flood of emotions, many of which are new to them, and they wear their emotions so close to the surface it's usually easy to see how they feel. They explode with rage, love, anger, joy, hopelessness, and longing, often over the course of a five-minute period.

It is my job (especially working with sixth graders, the youngest students at the school) to teach them how to handle these emotions and use them in a positive way. It took some time before I discovered that poetry is the perfect tool to channel their emotions. It is a means for them to express these new feelings that they don't have the vocabulary to express yet.

When I first started teaching poetry I focused on the rudiments of the craft: the stanza breaks, rhyme schemes, and imagery. I taught poetry for solely academic purposes, and I failed. The kids didn't make connections and didn't care about the poems. To them, poetry was so abstract and tedious to digest that it was like analyzing an ice cream sundae without ever enjoying the taste. They had been taught the small details without ever being given permission to enjoy the poem as a whole. More importantly, nobody ever showed them how to dislike a poem like a scholar.

I try to pair poetry with novels and other texts throughout the year, but we also devote quite a bit of time to poetry during National Poetry Month in April. Three years ago I was gearing up for National Poetry Month and I read an article by Brian Sztabnik on *Edutopia* outlining his March Madness novel brackets. This was the genesis for my plan to create the April Awesomeness Poetry Challenge.

I had the students fill out brackets anticipating which poem would win in a head-to-head vote and move on to the next round. These brackets then became the guide for some heated in-class discussions. Pitting two poems against each other gave the students an entry point into the poems. It's often difficult to explain what makes a poem great or terrible. It's much easier to explain why a poem is better or worse than another poem.

The poem debates gave the students freedom to express their love or hatred of the poems for any reason as long as they could defend it. I gave them basic analysis tools, but they taught me things about poetry I had never imagined.

April Awesomeness Poetry Challenge
LEARNING GOALS

BROAD **IMPLICATIONS**

Students will understand that:

- Poems take multiple readings to comprehend.
- Discussion can help develop a better understanding of a text.
- Evidence is necessary to defend a position.
- A negative opinion of a text is not a bad opinion if defended with evidence.

KNOWLEDGE GAINED

Students will know:

- Types of evidence to defend a position on a poem.
- The characteristics of a successful poem.

SKILLS ACQUIRED

Students will be able to:

- Take a position on a poem and support that position with evidence.
- Discuss a poem with peers and disagree respectfully.

EVIDENCE OF LEARNING

- The students will mark moments in the poem that stand out.

JOSHUA STOCK

- The students will complete the analysis guide to prepare for the discussion of the poem.

- The students will participate in a Socratic Circle discussing the value of the poems.

- The students will write a reflection piece explaining which poem was the most interesting/most successful, including evidence from the poem.

LEARNING PLAN

In a prior lesson students receive a copy of the poetry-bracket organizer along with a packet of the poems included in the bracket. The students are instructed to read each poem and decide which of them their classmates will choose as their favorite and write the title of the winning poem in the appropriate spots. The brackets are then brought back to class.

DAY 1:

- To begin the hour the teacher will explain "density" as it relates to science.

- The teacher will then connect the principle of density to the message being conveyed in a text. A novel has more words to spread the message out so it is less dense. A poem is usually more dense, because it has fewer words. Therefore poems require more readings to unpack.

- The teacher will have the students look at two rival poems on the poetry bracket.

- The teacher will read one of the poems once while the students listen.

- On the next reading the students will be instructed to mark any point in the poem that was interesting or confusing. A student volunteer will then read the poem to the class.

- On the third reading the students will be instructed to mark any word(s) in the poem that are interesting or boring. Another student volunteer will then read the poem to the class.

- The students will compare their notes with a partner.

- Then the students will complete a poetry analysis page regarding the poem.

- Steps 4-7 will be repeated with the second poem.

- Each student will make a final decision on which poem is the most successful.

DAY 2:

- The desks will be rearranged in a Socratic Circle with an inner circle and an outer circle.

- Students will work with a partner and discuss the following question: "What makes a poem successful?" They will write a list of qualities that make a poem successful.

- The whole class will discuss the question and come up with a couple of qualities that make a poem successful. If it isn't brought up, the teacher will encourage students to consider the purpose of the poem as a part of the definition of a successful poem.

- Both poems will be read aloud by the teacher.

- Both poems will also be read aloud by at least one student volunteer.

JOSHUA STOCK

- The inner circle will discuss which poem was the most successful and why. The outer circle will take notes of things they want to add or change to their opinion.

- After 5-7 minutes the groups will switch.

- At the end of the Socratic Circle, the students will write a paragraph explaining which poem was the most successful, and support that analysis with at least 2 examples from the text.

SUBSEQUENT DAYS:

The steps are repeated for the rest of the bracket. As the students progress, some of the steps are shortened or skipped. Also, the focus can change to allow for more discussion.

Possible alterations for later rounds of the bracket:

- Focus on imagery in the poems.

- Allow students to read the poem with different emotions to see if that affects which poem is more successful.

- Look at background information of the authors and discuss how that affects whether or not a poem is successful.

HANDOUTS/RESOURCES

- Bracket sample
- Analysis sample sheet
- Copies of the poems listed below:
  - "Masks" by Shel Silverstein
  - "Eating Poetry" by Mark Strand
  - "I Loved My Friend" by Langston Hughes
  - "Nothing Gold Can Stay" by Robert Frost
  - "Death of a Snowman" by Vernon Scannell

- "My Papa's Waltz" by Theodore Roethke
- "Fire and Ice" by Robert Frost
- "Dreams" by Langston Hughes
- "The Rose That Grew From Concrete" by Tupac Shakur
- "I Know Why the Caged Bird Sings" by Maya Angelou
- "If I Can Stop One Heart from Breaking" by Emily Dickinson
- "The Road Not Taken" by Robert Frost
- "Do Not Go Gentle into That Good Night" by Dylan Thomas
- "Kidnap Poem" by Nikki Giovanni
- "Wall Marks" by Shel Silverstein

JOSHUA STOCK

Poem Title: Caged Bird	Poem Title: The Rose That Grew From Concrete
How does this poem relate to YOUR life **OR** what message/moral does this poem teach you?	How does this poem relate to YOUR life **OR** what message/moral does this poem teach you?
Draw a picture of what you see when you read this poem.	Draw a picture of what you see when you read this poem.
Why do you think someone would like this poem?	Why do you think someone would like this poem?
What is one question someone might have about the poem? (what is this about? doesn't count)	What is one question someone might have about the poem? (what is this about? doesn't count)

"The Red Wheelbarrow" by William Carlos Williams

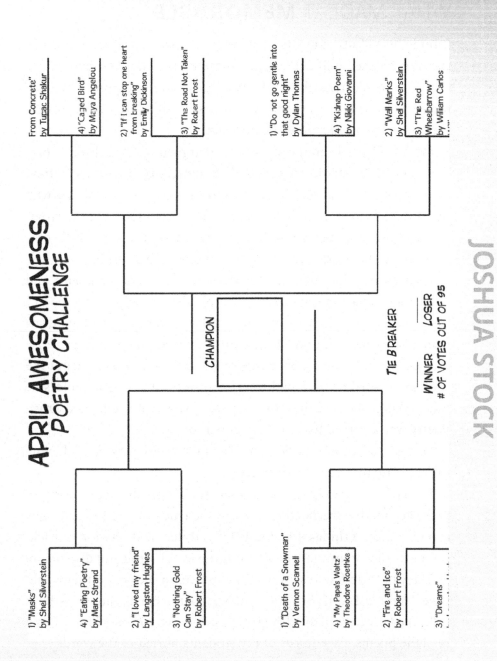

APRIL AWESOMENESS
POETRY CHALLENGE

JOSHUA STOCK

CHAMPION

TIE BREAKER

WINNER   LOSER

OF VOTES OUT OF 95

From Concrete"
by Tupac Shakur

4) "Caged Bird"
by Maya Angelou

2) "If I can stop one heart
from breaking"
by Emily Dickinson

3) "The Road Not Taken"
by Robert Frost

1) "Do not go gentle into
that good night"
by Dylan Thomas

4) "Kidnap Poem"
by Nikki Giovanni

2) "Wall Marks"
by Shel Silverstein

3) "The Red
Wheelbarrow"
by William Carlos

1) "Masks"
by Shel Silverstein

4) "Eating Poetry"
by Mark Strand

2) "I loved my friend"
by Langston Hughes

3) "Nothing Gold
Can Stay"
by Robert Frost

1) "Death of a Snowman"
by Vernon Scannell

4) "My Papa's Waltz"
by Theodore Roethke

2) "Fire and Ice"
by Robert Frost

3) "Dreams"

WHAT MADE IT **MEMORABLE**

I am in awe of my students every year. The way they look at poetry, the nuances they sniff out, and the evidence they use to support their assertions could rival those of any scholar. More importantly, I see the pride in their eyes when I can honestly tell them they've discovered something I had never heard before.

My awe comes from the student who argued that the three Robert Frost poems we studied spanned all of humanity from the creation, to life on Earth, and finally to the end of days. Or the student who decided William Carlos Williams's poem "The Red Wheelbarrow" was actually about being poor and the white chicken was all the narrator had in the world, and he loved it more than anything.

Even greater than that are the students who take the poems and make them a part of their lives. I had no idea of the power of poetry until we started this activity. The depth of emotions the kids draw from a few simple lines to share with their peers is beautiful.

I teach this lesson for kids like my student who ranted about the road she wished her dad had traveled instead of the poor choices he was making. She said that. In a tear-streaked vent she quoted Frost. Poetry was a part of her, a guide on her journey.

Or my student who ended the year by thanking me for believing in "this rose that grew from concrete."

Poetry is a great equalizer, and when kids get the opportunity to move beyond the mechanics, to get at the true heart of the text, they can do amazing things. I had kids from different ability levels, backgrounds, and circumstances all engaging in this beautiful discussion.

Many of them found a piece of themselves in the poems that would have been masked if they were limited to answering questions for a test. They, in turn, altered how I perceive the poems. Now, when I read the poems, I see traces of my students buried in the words.

JOSH STOCK *has spent the last seven years teaching middle school students in Olathe, KS in a wide range of language arts-related areas, including ninth grade English, Newspaper, Read 180, and most recently sixth grade Language Arts. He loves working with middle school students because of their creativity and fearlessness.*

Josh loves technology and has used that passion to merge technology with reading and writing instruction. He received a Masters degree in Instructional Design and Technology in 2010 from Emporia State University. Since then he has become an avid blogger, Twitter enthusiast and self-proclaimed awesomeness expert. In 2015 he presented at the MACE conference at Kansas State University, the International Society of Technology in Education national conference, and the National Council of Teachers of English national conference.

He is currently participating in action research with Kansas University on the use of technology to improve student writing and all around student awesomeness.

Follow him on Twitter @teachlikeaninja.

JOSHUA STOCK

When Novels Start with Bathroom Scenes

Dave Stuart, Jr.

"I first want students to realize how much we often miss on a first reading and then to see how delightfully confusing subsequent close readings of a passage can be. Students will analyze how one scene contributes to the book as a whole."

NO MATTER WHAT class I'm teaching — for the past five years, it's been a mixture of freshman World History and English 9 — my ultimate goal is the same: I want every minute in my classroom to be one that promotes the long-term flourishing of my students. For me, then, approaching Erich Maria Remarque's *All Quiet on the Western Front* is as much about grappling with the themes of one of the world's great novels as it is wrestling with what it takes to build a meaningful life. In this particular lesson, we hypothesize about the purpose of a seemingly incongruous scene from early on in the novel.

In one of the novel's early scenes, protagonist Paul sits in a meadow with a couple of his comrades-in-arms. Everything is pleasant about the scene — these friends are sitting in a circle, playing cards, laughing, talking — except for one jarring detail: they are sitting on boxes with holes in the tops and their pants are around their ankles. I always have my students read this chapter on their own prior to us reading it closely as a class, and it is amazing how few of my students catch what the soldiers are doing when they read it for the first time. As we read this passage closely, I enjoy watching my students' faces as, one after another, it dawns on them that these men are casually relieving their bowels together.

Now I told you that I teach freshmen, so you may be thinking, "Oh, great — ninth-grade-boy potty humor. Is the author of this chapter a moron?" And, I'll admit, the reason I love this lesson is partially because some of my kids always key in on how gross this scene is. You see, it's often those kids who are most changed by the lesson's end.

After reminding ourselves of this book's critical acclaim and of its longevity as a piece of world literature, we are faced with questions: Why this scene? Why here? Is Remarque *trying* to be vulgar? After hypothesizing answers to these questions in pairs and as a class, we re-read, this time with pencils in hand, noting any clues that may hint at an answer to our inquiry.

As we read the second time, students notice that there is even more unpleasantness in this scene than they first surmised. The characters refer to the proximity of the war front and a badly wounded person named Kemmerich. At some points, Paul and his friends have periods where they say nothing, leaving us to wonder what this silence reveals.

After we're finished with the second close reading, I have students ask three questions they're curious about — at this early point in the novel, we're looking less for answers than we are for better questions — and one of my key goals for the lesson is to provoke many students to wonder what on earth could have made these once-civilized young men become callous and crude, seeming to care more about getting double rations than they do about the deaths of half their company.

When Novels Start with Bathroom Scenes

LEARNING GOALS

BROAD **IMPLICATIONS**

Students will understand that:

- It is easy to miss entire layers of meaning on a first read.

- A novel's epigraph is an intentional part of any novel.

- When reading closely, it is helpful to adopt a particular question so as to focus one's reading.

KNOWLEDGE GAINED

Students will know:

- The definition and purpose of an epigraph.

- How novels can be most confusing for students in their initial chapters.

- That characters reveal themselves through what they do and don't say.

SKILLS ACQUIRED

Students will be able to:

- Closely read an excerpt of a novel from an objective stance, seeking to determine how one part of a novel relates to the whole.

- Use scene details to infer the purpose of a scene.

DAVE STUART, JR.

EVIDENCE OF LEARNING

- Students will quick-write to review details they remember from the previous day's reading.

- Students will work in pairs to review their previous day's reading.

- Students will closely read the scene from chapter one, this time using the lens of "What is odd about this scene?" Students will record "odd" details in their notebooks.

- Students will discuss their noticings with partners and the whole class.

- Students will closely read the scene a second time, this time in pursuit of structural and thematic questions, namely *Why this scene at this point in the novel?*

- Students will engage in a semi-structured, evidence-based, small group discussion.

- Students will reread the epigraph and conjecture about its relationship to today's scene.

- Students will reflect on what they've learned, both regarding the novel and regarding the reading process.

LEARNING PLAN

- The teacher will begin the period by having students open to a fresh sheet of their notebooks for a quick-write. The quick-write prompt is straightforward: "Thinking back to yesterday's reading of chapter one, write down 10 details that you can remember."

- The students will take turns sharing their details with their elbow partner.

- The teacher will ask the class how many of them wrote down anything about bathrooms during the quick write. The teacher will acknowledge responses and tell students to turn in their books to nearly the beginning of chapter one (look for "Today is especially good").

- The teacher tells the class to re-read from "Today is especially good" to "I wish he was here." Ask students to focus on one question: *What is odd about this scene?* The teacher tells students to keep track of anything they notice by writing notes in their notebooks.

- After five minutes, the teacher asks students to share their noticings with an elbow partner. The teacher then calls on students randomly to share what they noticed, keeping track of the discussion by writing responses in two categories on the board: ODD and QUESTIONS.

- One clear observation should be that the scene takes place in a makeshift, open-air circle of latrines, and that the men consider this very pleasant. The teacher asks the class what further questions this leaves them with. Ideal questions for continuing the lesson could be:

  - *Why does the author include this scene?*

  - *What happened to the men to make them so comfortable with such a "crude" thing?*

  - *Why does the author include this scene so early in the novel?*

- Armed with questions that fall along these lines, the teacher tells the students to go back and read closely, this time using one or more of the questions above as their lens.

DAVE STUART, JR.

- After five minutes, the teacher has students gather in groups of four to discuss what they noticed. Before the discussion, groups are given the following parameters:

  - Every person must speak at least once.

  - The text is king — every contribution should be rooted in something the text actually says or an inference drawn from something the text says.

- During the discussion, the teacher walks around and listens in, making note of misconceptions, great questions, and connections to the book's epigraph.

- When the discussion time limit has been reached (five minutes), the teacher brings the class back together. The teacher tells groups to "point nominate" someone to be their reporter (everyone points a finger at someone in the group; the person with the most fingers pointed at her is nominated), and groups report one interesting observation or question from their discussion.

- During reporting, the teacher is careful not to dole out answers. The beginnings of novels are places rife with questions; a key outcome of this lesson is that students will realize that this is normal and can even be enjoyable.

- If no group has referred back to the epigraph, the teacher asks students to re-read the epigraph. The teacher tells students to write three sentences about how the epigraph may help us understand Remarque's inclusion of this scene or its details at this point in the novel.

- If time remains, students again use their notebooks for a quick-write, this time to reflect on what they've learned in the lesson about both the novel and the reading process.

WHAT MADE IT **MEMORABLE**

So many of my students give up as soon as they encounter a challenging or confusing text because they believe that they are inadequate readers. They have the logic of fixed mindset: "this is hard, therefore I am dumb." What I love about this lesson is that, in a very non-razzle-dazzle fashion, it communicates to my students' hearts and minds that confusion is just a stone's throw away from insight because it can drive discerning questions. When our reading takes the stance of curiosity, it stands a chance of becoming joyful — even when we're reading a piece of literature written from across oceans of geography and time.

Additionally, I do have a heart for my freshman boys and their need to learn how to be both joyful and serious. The mere mention of bodily functions need not always lead to hysteria; by the end of this lesson, some of my goofiest guys have practiced the valuable life skill of restraining the impulse to make light of things, and this restraint guides them to writing profound end-of-lesson reflections.

DAVE STUART, JR *has taught in an urban middle school (Baltimore, MD), a rural high school (Cedar Springs, MI), and some of the richest and poorest schools in New York City since 2006. In all these settings, he has found that students everywhere enjoy learning how to be awesome at life, specifically in the areas of character and literacy. Conveniently, these areas are great predictors of life chances, and this is why Dave has enjoyed speaking with teachers about how to simultaneously simplify and amplify their approaches to teaching.*

Dave's writing at DaveStuartJr.com is read by over 35,000 people per month, and his accolades include a 2015 Teacher Innovator Grant from Character Lab, the 2014 Alumni Achievement Award from the

American College of Education, and recognition as a finalist for Michigan Teacher of the Year in 2015.

Follow him on Twitter @davestuartjr.

Think Like a Poet

Brian Sztabnik

"Perhaps the reason many students are turned off by poetry is because we make them read it rather than experience it. This lesson puts students in the mind of a poet. Without even realizing it, they will be analyzing the clues to determine its subject, imagery, point of view, and meaning. It is time they had a new experience with poetry, one where they think like a poet."

IT WAS MY second year at Miller Place, and just my fifth year of teaching overall, and I was taking over for everyone's favorite English teacher. Mr. Newcombe had taught for 30 years. His aura loomed large as he had won awards and completed numerous fellowships with the National Endowment for the Humanities. As he would often tell me, "This places students in the mindset of a poet."

I was assigned to take over his advanced courses and I did not want to let his students down, especially on the first day. I wanted to make an impression, and going over the syllabus and talking about course expectations just wasn't going to cut it.

I needed a way to show these senior students who I was, what the course would be about, and how we — together — could use literature to achieve something remarkable.

I turned to poetry.

As T. S. Eliot wrote, "Genuine poetry can communicate before it is understood," and for me, the poem that has always communicated with me is "Ulysses," by Alfred, Lord Tennyson.

I first read it in my early 20s. It was a formative time as I was trying to determine who I was, what I stood for, and what type of life I wanted to lead. Tennyson's words filled me with a fire to lead a life of purpose. It taught me to be a thinker and "follow knowledge like a sinking star beyond the utmost bounds of human thought." It warned me of the dangers of being passive: "how dull it is to pause, to make an end, to rust unburnish'd, not to shine in use!" It also encouraged me to never let a weakness cripple my will to achieve: "that which we are, we are;/ One equal temper of heroic hearts,/ Made weak by time and fate, but strong in will."

Time and time again I have returned to it, and its inspiration has never disappointed. I hoped, in turn, to use it to inspire them.

At 70 lines, it was too daunting for students to conquer in one 42-minute period. But there were 18 lines (see excerpt below) that would speak directly to them, as seniors about to embark on one last adventure.

I didn't want to be typical in any way. I didn't want to give them the poem, ask them to read it, and answer some questions. They deserved better of me.

I wanted them to experience the poem like they never had experienced one before. I wanted them to think like a poet, write like a poet, and talk like a poet. In doing so, they would read closely and analytically, although they wouldn't even realize they were doing it, because I wanted them so engrossed in what they were doing.

I wanted to show that in this course we would read complex, moving works of literature, we would grow to talk about them in sophisticated and nuanced ways, and we would experience them in personal ways, bringing ourselves into the literature and the literature into ourselves.

The result is "Think Like a Poet," a lesson in which I recite 18 lines from "Ulysses." They have to record it as I say it, and then work with a partner to try and recreate it as the poet wrote it. The students must think critically about how form contributes to meaning. As they examine the poem's words, they must weigh such poetic decisions as stanzas, line breaks, and rhythm.

It is my favorite lesson to teach.

Think Like a Poet
LEARNING GOALS

BROAD **IMPLICATIONS**

Students will understand that:

- If you think like a poet, you can read like a poet.

- Image clusters can reveal important qualities about the poem, such as the emotional state of its speaker, its setting, and its atmosphere.

- Shifts in tone are important markers in a poem's emotional curve that, when closely examined, lead readers to a complex understanding of a poem's movement.

- Iambic pentameter provides structure to a poem, influencing its rhythm and cadence.

- Old poems can be striking and new when readers reflect on their deeper truths.

KNOWLEDGE GAINED

Students will know:

- The characteristics of iambic pentameter.

- That the speaker of the poem is not necessarily the poet.

- That diction influences tone and tone influences mood.

- That poems have an emotional curve and rarely strike one note.

SKILLS ACQUIRED

Students will be able to:

- Read a poem with an analytical eye, recognizing how specific details and elements influence meaning.

- Use context clues to work through difficult areas of a poem.

EVIDENCE OF LEARNING

- Students will work in pairs to think like poets and write the section as the poet did, trying to re-create the line breaks, stanzas, and punctuation.

- The discussions each pair has will reveal their ability to think like poets.

- Their work, which will show the decisions they made, will reveal how they grappled with the poem.

- Their participation in the discussion about the poem will show their close-reading skills.

- For homework, students will have to find the complete poem, print it out, annotate it, and be prepared to discuss it in a Socratic Seminar for the next class.

LEARNING PLAN

- The teacher will begin the period by asking students to take out a sheet of paper or open to a clean page in their notebooks.

- The teacher will inform students that he will recite an excerpt, a powerful section from a much longer poem. Students will record the words of the excerpt as he recites them. They will not have the poem in front of them. They must re-create it on their own.

- Since this typically takes three recitations, the teacher will provide multiple readings from memory.

BRIAN SZTABNIK

- After three readings, the teacher will ask the students to get into pairs and try to recreate the excerpt as the poet wrote it. They must think like poets and consider such things as how stanza breaks, line length, and meter might allow the form to suit the function of the poem's excerpt.

- As the students work to recreate the excerpt, the teacher will circulate around the room and listen in on conversations, check their progress and offer some clues periodically that will be increasingly beneficial, such as: "this excerpt is one stanza," "it is 18 lines long," "it is written in iambic pentameter."

- The teacher will ask students to submit one copy that best reflects what they believe the section looked like originally.

- As a class, we will discuss what is revealed in the excerpt of the poem. It will start with a basic understanding:

  - *What are the dominant images? (Nautical ones).*

  - *Who is our speaker? (A seaman).*

  - *What do we know about him? (He is old and appears to be a leader of seamen).*

  - *What is his conflict? (Even though he is old, he wants one more adventure).*

  - *Can one really "sail beyond the sunset?" (Perhaps this is a metaphor for his desire to go beyond what we know of ourselves).*

  - *What is revealed of his character? (He is a brave, bold man who once fought valiantly, and even though he is old and not as strong as he once was, he wants to gather his men for one last adventure).*

- The teacher will close the period by reminding these high school seniors that even though they are the "old ones" in the building, they do not have to be idle, go through the motions, and coast their way through their senior year. "Some work of noble note may yet be done" and they have the potential to achieve beyond what they assume is possible.

- For homework, students will print out the rest of the poem, annotate it, and be prepared to discuss more about the poem's central figure in a Socratic Seminar for the next class.

HANDOUTS/RESOURCES

Materials

To be memorized and read aloud by the teacher:

"Ulysses"
Alfred, Lord Tennyson

There lies the port; the vessel puffs her sail:
There gloom the dark, broad seas. My mariners,
Souls that have toil'd, and wrought, and thought with me—
That ever with a frolic welcome took
The thunder and the sunshine, and opposed
Free hearts, free foreheads—you and I are old;
Old age hath yet his honour and his toil;
Death closes all: but something ere the end,
Some work of noble note, may yet be done,
Not unbecoming men that strove with Gods.
The lights begin to twinkle from the rocks:
The long day wanes: the slow moon climbs: the deep

Moans round with many voices. Come, my friends,
'T is not too late to seek a newer world.
Push off, and sitting well in order smite
The sounding furrows; for my purpose holds
To sail beyond the sunset, and the baths
Of all the western stars, until I die.

WHAT MADE IT **MEMORABLE**

It's no secret that many students struggle with poetry. They chafe against it because they have notions that it's obscure, dense, and best left in the past.

This lesson flips those notions upside down.

My students see poetry from the other side. They see it not as an abstract thing that they are being forced to read; they finally experience it as a poet does. They must tackle the myriad decisions that a poet faces, they must make sense of the speaker's point of view and how that may differ from the poet's, and they will see that a close examination of something that may be so foreign to them — an aging captain seeking one last sailing voyage — can touch something inside them and open up the possible for a spectacular senior year.

What better poem to do that than "Ulysses," Tennyson's dramatic monologue, which explores Odysseus' frustration with the static life of a king? It awakens something in all of us. No matter the stage of life, we can still produce "some work of noble note."

I love conveying this philosophy to my seniors at the beginning of the year. For them, it is a time when many have thoughts about coasting through the year, with their sights set on the traditional senior-year rites of passage — homecoming, college acceptances, the prom, and graduation. This excerpt refocuses their attention on the possibility for them to achieve something remarkable before the year is done. It encourages a deep conviction for some worthy pursuit, belief in the nobility of work, and an adventurous spirit in pursuit of something beyond expectation.

BRIAN SZTABNIK *has taught English for a little over a decade in New York. By day he shares his love of literature with his students, marks papers, plans lessons, and tries not to trip over backpacks in the aisle. By night he is a father, Twitter chat host, podcaster, and blogger.*

At the heart of everything that he does, though, is the belief that great ideas should be shared and celebrated. This simple principle has catapulted his podcast to No.1 in the K-12 category on iTunes. And it has enabled his writings to appear on Edutopia, Teaching Channel, EdWeek, Heinemann, and the AFT. He won the Educators Voice Award in 2015 for Education Commentator/Blogger, given out by the Academy of Education Arts and Sciences.

Follow him on Twitter @talkswteachers.

The Excitement Graph

Heather Wolpert-Gawron

*"I want students to walk away with a sense of what
jazzes them about a particular story or book and
then recognize that narratives generally have patterns
of writing that lead them to feel that way at certain
points of the storytelling. They will analyze the plot
structure in a narrative by literally plotting symbols
on a graph to indicate their level of excitement
during different parts of the tale. The resulting line
that can be drawn between these symbols should
indicate the 'story swoop' of the narrative."*

I AM A SECOND career teacher. My 20s were a bit of a lost decade, as I had held a series of jobs in the entertainment industry, but never really loved them. I spent that decade as a clock-watcher, and that didn't sit well with me. In my late 20s, I finally reflected on what would make me happy. I thought about what I liked to do, what I liked to talk about, what my strengths were, and even what I liked to wear. I was shocked to find that all the arrows I hadn't been interpreting pointed to teaching.

To make sure that my instinct was correct, I didn't leave my job in publicity right away. Instead, I tentatively signed up for a class in the UCLA Extension catalogue called "Teaching Reading for Elementary Students." At only 5-feet tall, I figured that if I were to become a teacher, then I needed clients much shorter than I was. Once I began teaching, however, and I had jumped into the secondary pool, I learned that middle schoolers were more my speed. Their energy, their spontaneous outbursts, their uncontrollable clumsiness due to growth-spurts that happened by the hour, the absolutely craziness of middle school, that was for me.

Anyway, back to that first education class. I figured if I liked it, I might be onto something. If I hated it, well then, back to the drawing board to figure out what I was supposed to be doing with my life.

Needless to say, I loved it. In hindsight, I got lucky. It could have been just like any other education class, a hoop to jump through for those who already had a goal in sight. But this course introduced me to concepts of how we learn using methods I had never considered before. Of course, I knew what had engaged me, a mediocre K-12 student at best, but I had never thought before to deconstruct the strategies that moved me. The class introduced me to the concept of different learning styles. It introduced me to subject matter integration. It introduced me to facts about brain development and the science of implementation. And it introduced me to a one-shot lesson using a strategy called *The Excitement Graph.*

I think the purpose of the lesson that was presented that one day was really to show us how to get students to think about adjectives and gradations of word choice. But what I came away with was a lesson that I have since tweaked and evolved and made a necessary part of every start-of-the-year lesson on plot structure.

Once I was given my own classroom, I immediately began using *The Excitement Graph,* and I have since used it every year. One year, it became a foldout in the students' writer's notebooks. In another, it took up a whole wall, complete with yarn graph lines and pinned symbols that moved with every debate and discussion.

When I taught fourth grade and fifth grade, I used this strategy when introducing students to great picture books such as David Shannon's *Nicolas Pipe* or Patricia Polacco's *Pink and Say.* When I taught credit recovery for high school, we produced *Excitement Graphs* through the lenses of both Shakespeare and Dickens. As a current middle school teacher, I have used them for such short stories as Gary Soto's "Seventh Grade" and Toni Cade Bambara's "The War of the Wall." It's an activity that brings in so much discussion and so many different angles of looking at plot structure that it speaks to many different kinds of students and many different levels of literature.

And here's something else I've found helpful: once I use it with the whole class at the beginning of the school year, I can generally use it later on as an informal assessment of an individual student. I can ask students to create *Excitement Graphs* to assess their understanding of the plot and pacing of stories throughout the school year. One year, I even had students produce them for every story and novel we read.

For nostalgia's sake, I'm going to show you *The Excitement Graph* using a picture book that I personally love and have used to teach students of all ages. It is also the one that was used all those years ago in that summer UCLA class. It also has an obvious climax — I like introducing students to *The Excitement Graph* using its recognizable structure before asking them to produce one independently based on more subtle storylines. Ladies and gentlemen, I present to you a great book: *The Three Little Wolves and the Big, Bad Pig.*

The Excitement Graph
LEARNING GOALS

BROAD **IMPLICATIONS**

Students will understand that:

- Plot structure can be predictable even while plot can be unique.

- Symbols can represent different elements within a narrative, such as character, main idea, theme, sensory detail.

- Graphing devices can be used to plot story points as variables.

- There are gradations of words that are specific in description and are not necessarily synonymous.

- Picture books can help to simplify the process of learning narrative no matter the student's age.

- Reflecting on plot is vital to understanding the nature of narrative.

- Different sections of a story will capture a reader's attention more than others.

- Being able to summarize the story in different sections of plot helps a reader to embed that overall plot more firmly.

KNOWLEDGE GAINED

Students will know:

- What a symbol is.

- How to plot X and Y coordinates on a graph.

- The sections of a traditional plot layout (exposition, rising action, climax, falling action, resolution).

SKILLS ACQUIRED

Students will be able to:

- Develop a list of words that emanate from a starting point of "good."

- Chart symbols relating to a story on a graph.

- Summarize the parts of a story that represent plot structure.

EVIDENCE OF LEARNING

- Students display a list of graduated words that range from worst to best, and can justify their decisions verbally.

- Students create an arch that identifies their interest level in a particular part of the plot. This arch indicates a story sequence as well as an analysis of that narrative plotline.

- Students select a symbol to represent the overall story. It will reflect character, theme, main idea, or conflict.

LEARNING PLAN

- The teacher will read aloud from the book *The Three Little Wolves and the Big, Bad Pig*. Students of all ages will be excited that "it's story time!"

- Following the reading, students will be given graph paper (hard copy or digital).

- The teacher will lead a discussion about symbolism.

- Students will decide independently on the symbol that best represents the story. Such possibilities might include a pig head, a teapot, a house, etc.

- Thinking about typical elements of plot structure, students will divide the X-axis (horizontal) into an agreed number of

HEATHER WOLPERT-GAWRON

sections. For instance, if the class decides that there is only one plot point related to each of the following: exposition, rising action, climax, falling action, resolution, then the class would divide the labels of their horizontal lines into only five sections. However, if the class decides that there might be multiple moments that contribute to, say, rising action, then you may have somewhere between 7-10 sections labeling the X-axis on the graph.

- Students will, independently and in their own words, summarize each of the sections and write them as labels for the X-axis.

- The teacher will lead a discussion about gradations of word choice. The teacher will point to the middle of the Y-axis line and tell students that they are going to brainstorm "excitement" words in degrees to go up the line. What they want to end up with is a vertical line that has the word that describes the lowest level of excitement on the bottom and the highest level of excitement on the top. The teacher should set standards for the types of adjectives by eliminating blah words like "OK," "Bad," "Fine." Having said that, however, you need to set the mid-line. The teacher should label the mid-point "good." I know, I know, it's a blah word, but it's a starting point. It's the last blah word you'll allow.

- Students will copy "good" and its placement on the graph in front of them.

- Now students should shout out words that mean "better than good." They should be thrown/written as a splash or brainstorm of suggestions. The teacher can introduce students to VisualThesaurus so that they can research word choices and meanings before spewing them into the discussion. If a teacher would rather the students use a more digital way to creating a collaborative word wall, he or she can develop a *Padlet* link or *Google* Doc and share it with the students.

- The class now must rank those words moving up from "good"according to intensity. Which of them represents what we as readers find the most interesting?

- Enter the words in order from "good" to whatever word they decided meant the best. Perhaps it is "stupendous," or "magnificent," or something like that.

- Now, starting again with "good," have students brainstorm gradations of lack of interest. That is, what negative words describe how they feel about the least interesting part of the book? Perhaps it is something like "horrendous."

- Once the negative words are sorted, the teacher and students should have a graph that has summarized sections listed across the X-axis and a list of words from something like "horrendous" to "stupendous" running up the Y-axis.

- Students will now plot their symbols on the graph to reflect the level of interest for each summarized description of the story. These results will, nine times out of ten, look a lot like a typical "story arch." You'll find that in a typical narrative swoop, the beginning will, in the opinion of the students, start at around the "good" or "mediocre" level for the exposition. This will most likely, if they liked the overall story, rise to something like "stupendous" for the climax and fall back to "mediocre" by the time they get to the resolution.

- Teachers can follow up with the fact that not all stories follow the same arch. Show them the digital resource from ReadWriteThink: http://www.readwritethink.org/files/resources/interactives/plot-diagram/

HEATHER WOLPERT-GAWRON

- This diagram allows students not only to separate plot points into different beats along a narrative arch, or to see variations of the narrative arch, but also to adjust the *Graph* according to where the climax occurs. They can concretely see what a cliffhanger or a story that does not follow the typical "bell curve" plot structure looks like.

EXTENSION ACTIVITY:

- Besides having students use *Excitement Graphs* to help analyze the story arch for narratives they have read, they can also be used for feedback on the students' writing. Once a student produces a rough draft of a narrative, he or she can then reflect and design an *Excitement Graph*. Then, have the students swap narratives and produce a *Graph* for someone else's story. Have the students compare the *Graphs* they created from the stories they wrote to the *Graphs* their peers made after reading their stories. Did the reader feel moved in appropriate places? Did the reader recognize all the elements of the story in the summary? An *Excitement Graph*, therefore, can act as a feedback device to help drive revisions.

HANDOUTS/ RESOURCES

Excitement Graph

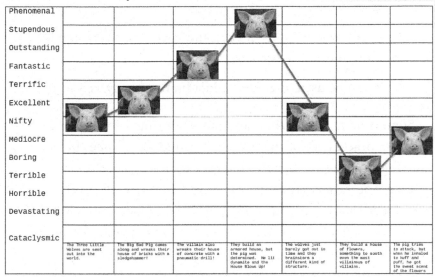

ReadWriteThink: http://www.readwritethink.org/files/resources/
interactives/plot-diagram/VisualThesaurus

WHAT MADE IT **MEMORABLE**

This activity is one that I have done with third graders through twelfth graders. Its sweet spot, however, is third through eighth grades. For high school, it is engaging because it is cross-curricular, but it is not challenging enough for those who already understand storylines and word choice. Nevertheless, even high schoolers like to whip out the crayons every now and then to get goofy, and any way to bring some lighthearted activity to the rigorous act of analyzing text is legitimate. Can you imagine what an *Excitement Graph* would look like if it were done based on *To Kill A Mockingbird* or *Macbeth*? What would a hero's journey look like versus a cliffhanger? The level of literature can help determine the lesson's level.

For elementary and middle school, however, this lesson can serve many purposes:

HEATHER WOLPERT-GAWRON

- it can be used for whole class brainstorming;

- it can be used for independent homework for an informal assessment;

- it can be developed in class and used as a study tool for a more formal assessment;

- it can be used as evidence in a literary analysis.

Summarizing, analyzing, and story writing — this lesson helps students practice all of these skills. I would also argue that students could use persuasive writing to justify their decisions.

I have never met students who didn't engage with this lesson, but remember that when you conduct it, its goof-factor should be offset with the rigor of the literature and the language level you require from the students.

Anything fun can be made rigorous with modeling and expectations. Have fun graphing your literature.

HEATHER WOLPERT-GAWRON *is an award-winning middle school teacher who also writes her popular education blog as Tweenteacher. She is a staff blogger for Edutopia and a fellow of the National Writing Project.*

Heather tells her students that she is not a language arts teacher, but rather, a teacher in the art of using language. She believes that her role as a writing teacher is to help students elevate how to communicate any content, not just literature. She helps students write, speak, record, construct, and produce presentations.

She tells stories through curriculum, and her students play a role in the telling of them.

She has authored three series of workbooks: Internet Literacy for grades 3-8, *Project Based Writing, grades 3-8, and Nonfiction Reading Strategies for the Common Core, grades 1-7. She is also the author of DIY Project Based Learning for ELA and History and DIY Project Based Learning for Math and Science (2015) all written for Routledge Publishing.*

Follow her on Twitter @Tweenteacher.

HEATHER WOLPERT-GAWRON

CPSIA information can be obtained
at www.ICGtesting.com
Printed in the USA
LVOW13s1920280717
542953LV00010B/76/P

9 780692 531556